DISABLED PARENTS
Dispelling the Myths

DISABLED PARENTS
Dispelling the Myths

Michele Wates

A
NATIONAL CHILDBIRTH TRUST
GUIDE

Published by National Childbirth Trust Publishing
in association with Radcliffe Medical Press

N C T
PUBLISHING

Other Titles Published by NCT Publishing:

BEING PREGNANT, GIVING BIRTH
Mary Nolan

BECOMING A FAMILY
Anna McGrail

BREASTFEEDING YOUR BABY
Jane Moody, Jane Britten and Karen Hogg

WORK AND HOME
Teresa Wilson

NEW GENERATIONS: 40 YEARS OF BIRTH IN BRITAIN
Joanna Moorhead

Published by National Childbirth Trust Publishing,
25–27 High Street, Chesterton, Cambridge CB4 1ND, UK
in association with Radcliffe Medical Press.

© 1997 NCT Publishing.
First published 1997.

A CIP catalogue record for this book is available from the British Library.

ISBN 1-85775-257-0

Picture Acknowledgements
The publishers would like to thank the following for their permission to
reproduce photographs:
Cover: picture of Lydia Thomas and her son Jamie by Charlotte Winn.
Geoff Sayer: pp8, 11, 38, 52, 101, 116; Brenda Prince/Format: pp19, 73,
128, 138; David Hevey: p29; Amanda Knapp: p86.
Illustrations: Peter Froste.

Design by Tim McPhee.
Production in association with Book Production Consultants plc,
25–27 High Street, Chesterton, Cambridge CB4 1ND, UK.

Printed by The Alden Press, Osney Mead, Oxford

For David and Anna

'. . . *disabled parents . . . coming out of the secret places which non-disabled people know nothing of, becoming visible within society, proud and strong because we have dared to believe that love is more important than muscle.*'

Micheline Mason

THE NATIONAL CHILDBIRTH TRUST offers information and support in pregnancy, childbirth and early parenthood, and aims to enable every parent to make informed choices. The NCT is working towards ensuring that its services, activities and membership are fully accessible to everyone. Donations to support our work are welcome.

Contents

Publisher's note

COMMENTS and personal accounts were given to us in confidence, so out of respect for our contributors' privacy we have changed some names.

We have endeavoured where possible to reproduce quotations verbatim, but where editing has been applied, the integrity of the quotation has been maintained.

About the author

Michele Wates is a writer, researcher and a disabled mother. Over the past eight years she has been involved in the growth of a peer support and campaigning network amongst disabled parents which she considers is a vitally important facet of the empowerment of disabled people.

Acknowledgements

I am grateful to Colin Fletcher for getting me started on this piece of writing and for countless discussions on the subject of families and parenting; some theoretical, some personal, some practical and some completely impractical but good fun, which is why in our family we still tend to refer to him as either Colin the Motorbike or Playdough Colin (the faint pink mark on the kitchen ceiling tells its own story!). Thanks also to Colin's erstwhile colleagues at the once unique and now defunct Department of Social Policy at Cranfield Institute of Technology, who continued to support me in my desire to write a book, even when it was clear that I was no longer interested in writing a thesis.

My thanks to the following for their thoughtful reading of various versions of the text and for moral support: Tim and Wendy Booth, Vic Finkelstein, Mukti Jain Campion, Gill Howe, Deidre Macfarlane, Mike Nicholson, Micheline Mason, Jo O'Farrell, Katherine Stott and Edward Wates.

A special mention is due to Peter Hutchinson who talked me through the early days of learning to use my lap-top computer and was consistently and ungrudgingly generous with advice over the phone.

My heartfelt thanks and sincere appreciation to all the mothers and fathers who shared their time and insights with me and in whose company I am proud to be a disabled parent. I am privileged to share with them, and all my co-workers in ParentAbility, the rich experience of bringing about change.

And finally thank you to my very special family, the ones I live with and the ones further afield, for being there.

Introduction

WHY WRITE ABOUT DISABLED PARENTS?

'Becoming a parent is the best thing that ever happened to me. I still feel, although it was eight years ago, that I snatched at something I didn't have a right to.'

Micheline Mason[1]

The number of disabled parents appears to be on the increase. Developments in medical technology mean that many individuals born with impairments, who fifty years ago would not have been expected to reach child-bearing age, are now surviving to adulthood and many impairment specific organisations report an increase in enquiries from prospective parents.

The NHS & Community Care Act of 1990 accelerated a reduction in the numbers of disabled people living in residential 'homes', hospitals and hostels, so that there are currently fewer disabled people living under institutional supervision than at any time since the nineteenth century. Whereas a young, severely disabled adult living in residential care might not have been expected to develop sexual relationships and might indeed have been actively *deterred* from child-bearing,[2,3,4,5] young disabled adults living in the community might be more likely to form sexual partnerships and to think of themselves as having the right to experience a range of relationships, including that of parent. However, Jenny Morris also reminds us that some young disabled people 'in the community' live under the gaze of over-protective parents. Some of the people she interviewed in the process of preparing her book on independent living had actually chosen to go into residential care in the hope of achieving a greater degree of freedom![6]

In addition to any actual increase in numbers there is an increase in the *visibility* of disabled parents as they become a more noticeable group.[7] Disabled people who became parents and parents who became disabled often kept a low profile in the past in order not to attract attention and possible negative intervention. Many still feel that it is not safe to put their heads above the parapet, for there is still ample evidence of a lack of confidence in disabled people's ability to parent.[8,9]

The first question many disabled women find themselves being asked when they say that they intend to have a baby is, 'Are you sure you can cope?'. Perhaps it is not surprising, given that most medical and social welfare professionals are so used to seeing disabled people as patients and clients first and foremost that they find it hard to imagine someone with a disability being responsible for a dependent baby. More surprisingly perhaps, there are frequent reports of family members and friends trying to put disabled women off having children.

The objections raised are often practical in nature: 'How are you going to pay for the extra help and equipment?'; 'How are you going to carry the baby?'; 'What will happen if your condition gets worse?'. Sometimes underlying the practical objections is a barely concealed prejudice on the part of the person objecting. 'My sister, when finding out I was pregnant, said I should have been sterilised before I was 18, as I obviously couldn't control my own fertility and I shouldn't have children. She didn't speak to me from that day until the baby was four days old . . .'.[10]

Disability is so closely associated with dependence and social isolation that it is hard for people to imagine a disabled individual at the centre of family life in the role of primary carer.[11]

One can only guess at the numbers of disabled women and men who had a strong desire to become parents but never did so because they had internalised messages of doubt and disapproval from those around them. Some never felt that they could become parents; others were dissuaded at an early stage, some were persuaded to terminate wanted pregnancies.

Occasionally there are reports of direct intervention in the reproductive lives of disabled women through enforced sterilisation, the refusal of fertility treatment on the grounds of disability and even enforced abortions.[12] Some disabled parents have found themselves fighting social services departments to be allowed to take their new babies home from hospital.

Disabled women who become mothers against a background of scepticism and disapproval sometimes report that they felt under pressure to try to be 'supermums' in order to demonstrate their competence. There can be a corresponding temptation to keep any difficulties that are experienced hidden for fear of having children removed from home. 'Disabled people themselves face pressure from society to be "model parents". Scarce resources and a lack of information add to this pressure – and families who fear their child will be taken into care are unwilling to let professionals know they need help'.[13]

What is more widespread and in many ways more undermining than open hostility is the general lack of expectation that disabled people will become parents. The numbers of disabled parents are unknown and have to be guessed at because originators of official statistics have never thought to correlate *disability* with *parenthood* and thus the relevant questions have never been asked. Disabled people who attended 'special' schools as children consistently report that, where they received sex education at all, this covered contraception but no mention of parenthood (see Chapter Three). Hospitals whose facilities for disabled people are exemplary in every other respect have given little or no thought to disabled access in the maternity ward.[14]

For the most part these exclusions are unconscious; all the

same they convey to disabled people that their presence is not expected in the domain of pregnancy, birth and parenthood. When I told people I was researching the subject of disabled parents I noticed that people often thought I was talking about *parents of disabled children.*

A few publications in recent years have given out a different message by setting the issues and practicalities facing disabled parents centre-stage.[15,16,17,18] In addition, a number of books have touched on the issues facing disabled parents as part of the experience of disabled people[19,20,21] or as part of exploring parenting issues.[22,23] The Spinal Injuries Association has produced two children's stories of everyday family life in which the parents happen to be wheelchair users.[24]

The question 'Are you sure you can cope?' may be insensitive but the concern behind it is genuine. *Disabled Parents: Dispelling the Myths* is not a book about heroines, not an account of a group of problem parents, nor yet an attempt to show that disabled parents are perfectly normal really when you get to know them. It is a response to that concern. Here is an opportunity to listen whilst disabled parents describe just how they do cope, what they value in their parenting, the barriers they face, what they find helpful and unhelpful in terms of support from a range of sources and what they hope to achieve by working together.

JOINING FORCES

When I asked disabled parents to tell me about their lives I did not realise the effect this would have on my own life – the more I tried to move towards the horizon, the further it expanded, until what looked like a neat, self-contained two-year-study became a veritable life project; fast-moving, large scale and increasingly complex. What began for me as talks with other parents with limited mobility in my area became part of a larger story about mutual support and self-determination amongst disabled parents on a national scale.

It is right that these two perspectives, the personal and the collective, should be brought together in one book, for the strength of the group arises out of individuals finding their voices, sharing stories and seeing in the common strands both what needs changing and the possibilities for joining forces.

I have not written *Disabled Parents: Dispelling the Myths* with any one type of reader in mind; I hope that it is a book which parents and professionals alike will find interesting and useful.

The second part of the book describes how disabled parents, and disabled mothers in particular, have taken a lead in developing a network of peer support and fostering improvements in the services and support available to disabled parents. This is very much 'work in progress' rather than a finished story and the book ends by identifying what is being learnt currently about how disabled parents can be supported and empowered in their attempts to bring about change.

LEARNING FROM DISABLED PARENTS

It is clear from some of the issues raised in the latter part of the book that some disabled parents face serious difficulties brought about by under-resourcing on the one hand and prejudice on the other. This was disturbingly illustrated by an edition of *Face the Facts* broadcast on Radio 4 (June 14 1995) in which the cases of two children who had been forcibly removed from their disabled parents were discussed. The accounts of parenting in the first part of this book reveal a group of parents whose confidence was on the whole high and whose competence had rarely been brought into question, whatever doubts might have been expressed to some of them when they first announced that they were pregnant.

Whilst some people might criticise the book because it does not deal with situations in which there were felt to be substantial difficulties, I regard it as a strength. It underlines a fact that is easily overlooked in studies that are based on 'problem' cases – that generally speaking, people, and this includes disabled people, are resourceful in finding ways around the challenges they face. Disabled parents have a strong sense of themselves as regular parents dealing as others do with the ups and downs of family life. Disability and the barriers to participation do figure strongly but without detracting from the sense of satisfaction in doing the job.

There clearly are issues to address where support breaks down and increasingly attention is being given to this (see Chapter Ten). It is important to view the findings from my own study against the background of those concerns and to consider instances where things have gone wrong in the light of such everyday accounts as these.

My aim in writing is not to show how wonderful it is to be a disabled parent since disabled mothers, and fathers too, are amongst those most severely affected by the under-resourcing, poor moral support, unwelcoming attitudes and inappropriate physical design which to a greater or lesser extent affect the lives of all parents in our society. In addition, these things will go on affecting disabled parents as disabled *people* even after their children have grown.

American disability rights activist, Marca Bristo, at a Policy Studies Institute conference, spoke powerfully of barriers she had encountered as a disabled parent.

> *'I am at a museum in Chicago, a museum that has just built a brand new major department; my child, my two-year-old, climbs down off my lap, runs off across the room, a crowd comes between me and the child and I hear my child crying: "mommy, mommy, mommy". I rush to get my child as any mother would do, to be greeted by five stairs that were built subsequent to the laws that said you should not build stairs in new contexts. I could not get to my son. Ultimately a stranger brought him back to me, put him on my lap and we went on home. That was the*

day in my life, although I dedicated my life to removing barriers, that I got as mad as hell and said, "I'm not going to take it any more". Those barriers, they are not barriers, they are acts of discrimination; they are wrong and they do not need to be there. When I filed my complaint under a city ordinance, the man screamed at me over the telephone, the most undignified way I have ever been treated, as he said, "Mrs Bristo, I hardly know what to say to you about your inability to care for your own children". Fundamentally, those stairs are about the same prejudice that believes I should not have those children because I am not capable of caring for them.'[25]

Those who are hardest hit by challenges are often those who have gone furthest towards finding solutions. For this reason the experience of disabled parents is profoundly relevant to all parents and to those who work with them.

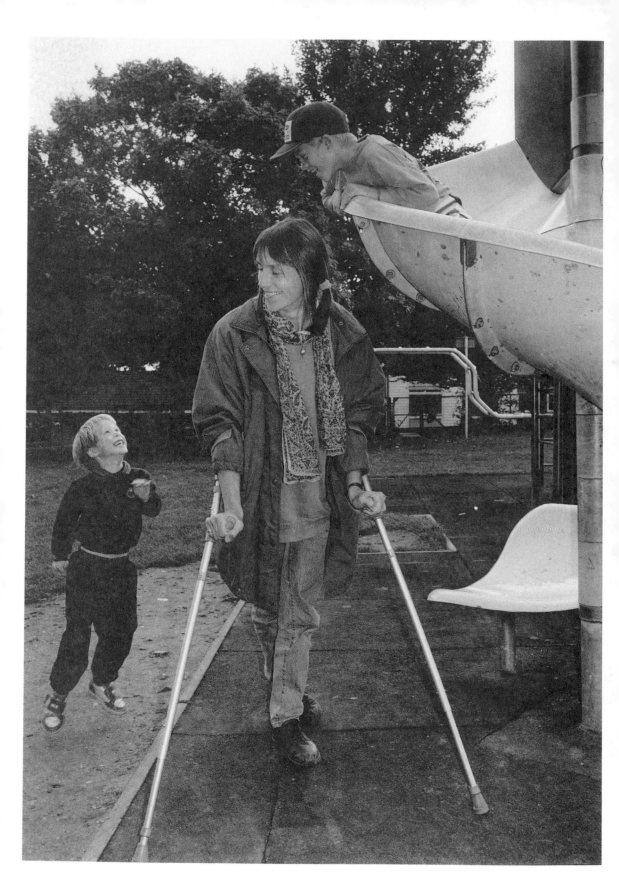

CHAPTER ONE

Not Another Book About Heroines

A PERSONAL STARTING POINT

*'I hope this isn't going to be another of those books
about heroines.'*

Sally

When I was first diagnosed, at the age of 27, as having
multiple sclerosis, my doctor put me in touch with a
woman of my own age who had the same illness and had
recently had her first child. She became a good friend and
through her I came to know another woman with older
children, who had also been recently diagnosed.

When I was thinking about whether I myself would become a
mother and later, after my first child was born, it was extremely
useful to be able to share my hopes and fears with these women
friends and listen as they talked about their own experiences.
However, I did not seek further contacts or information and it
never occurred to me to find out whether any specific support
was available to disabled parents, either from statutory
authorities or through the voluntary sector.

If offers of support had been made, I might not have taken
them up in any case, since like many disabled people, I was
keen to blend in as far as possible with the 'able-bodied'. Up to
this point I had never been part of any organisation or support
group which had disability as its focus, and this was in part
because I felt uncomfortable about thinking of myself as a
disabled person.

Whilst I was deciding whether or not to have a second child I began to feel that, in spite of this reluctance, it might be interesting to make contact with other disabled parents. The effects of the illness upon me were becoming more apparent as my walking became increasingly laboured and erratic and the likelihood was that it would continue to worsen. I had to consider the practical difficulties that might arise if I had another child to deal with. How would I feel about my increasing need for support? How would I respond to any suggestion that I was being less than responsible in having a second child?

I had the feeling, without being able to say exactly where it came from, that disabled mothers were assumed to be 'problem' mothers, or 'at risk' in some way. Yet my own limited experience and observation suggested to me that there are certain distinctive *strengths* in the parenting styles of disabled people. A growing interest in meeting and talking with other parents dealing with similar issues and challenges to those I faced, coincided with an interest in posing a question that seemed not to have been asked before – 'In what ways do disabled people make particularly good parents?'.

For example, I had noticed that I found it necessary, and therefore natural, to involve other adults and young people in the day-to-day tasks of looking after and entertaining my son. This made parenting a more companionable experience for me and at the same time gave him positive and playful interactions with people beyond the immediate family. I was interested to know whether other disabled parents found the same.

So far so good. My research would be a celebration of the distinctive qualities of disabled parents and would also identify some of the common challenges faced. My plan was to make contact with other parents with limited mobility and who had young children and lived in the same area as myself; my peer group, so to speak. Later, I hoped, we might have the opportunity to meet together for discussion and mutual support.

It soon became clear that it was going to be much harder than I had thought to find other parents to talk with. I contacted three parents already known to me, and through two of them, found two more. Two chance meetings led to interviews. However, attempts to make further contacts by means of a letter to the local paper, a short interview on local radio and letters to a number of local disability support groups were all unproductive.

The difficulty of making contact made me aware of the low visibility of disabled parents. Were they not actually getting out and about all that much? Was word of my search not getting through or did they prefer not to identify themselves? The lack of success in making contact through voluntary groups also raised the question as to whether disabled parents tend to distance themselves from such networks.

At the same time as pursuing informal contacts I worked my way slowly and steadily through a protocol which would enable me to approach health and social service personnel directly. It seemed safe to assume that every member of the sample group would at some point come into contact with one or more services. In the event, although the process was lengthy and laborious (for example, the local Research Ethics Committee required no fewer than 17 copies of my draft questionnaire!) I was finally able to send letters to GPs and health visitors and also to get word of the research through to social workers. In due course these approaches led to meetings with 13 more parents.

In addition to the difficulty of making contact, the wind was further knocked out of my sails in the course of my first interview with another disabled mother. I had explained that I hoped to write my findings up in a book. Sally said dubiously, 'I hope this isn't going to be another of those books about heroines'. On reflection I took her point. The media loves to present the lives of disabled people in terms of their exceptionality: their bravery and determination in the face of

adversity and tragedy. There is also a contrasting, but equally marked tendency, to *blame* disabled people for their irresponsibility in having children whom they may not be considered able to look after without assistance.

The apparent contrast between praising and blaming is not as great as it seems since the effect of both approaches is to distance the experience of disabled parents from that of their non-disabled counterparts. I was finding, and this was supported by other research,[1] that disabled parents did not wish to be singled out, whether for praise, blame or sympathy; that they were not interested in having a special place on the margins of society but saw themselves as 'normal' parents getting on with the job they had chosen to do. Tensions emerged between standing out and blending in, between celebration and blame, between letting needs be known and keeping them hidden.

As the interviews progressed the word 'normal' cropped up so frequently that it seemed to be a kind of cipher, indicating something beyond itself. Normality was seen as something positive and desirable. It was not the midpoint between a rich, full life on the one hand and an impoverished, reduced one on the other. It had lost any connotation of mediocrity and taken on the significance of an ideal.

It was important to this group of parents to have the 'normality' of their experience acknowledged by others and to affirm their sense of it in themselves and their families. What is 'normal'? Who can say what a 'normal family' is and does? And yet the concept was clearly so important that it required exploration.

Disabled parents are not alone in the importance which they attach to the indefinable concept of normality. Many writers see achieving 'normality' as the goal of sick and disabled people and their families.[2,3] What they fail to recognise is that unquestioning acceptance of this view helps to keep in place the assumption that the experience of disabled people is inherently *abnormal*.

Disabled people cannot help but absorb the message that

disability is equated with abnormality and abnormality with malfunction. The perception is that providers of health and social services operate on the basis of these same assumptions and from there the association is easily made between being seen as different and being seen as problematic. And so, from a disabled parent's point of view, doing one's best to appear normal may seem like the safest route to a family life free from unwelcome intervention. Asserting one's 'normality' is linked ultimately with asserting the right to retain control of one's life.

There can come a point however where the concept of normality becomes tyrannical in its effect on a disabled person's life, demanding adherence to what is considered 'able-bodied' behaviour, whether or not it is appropriate, and making any concessions to the reality of impairment feel like failure. Ironically, the results can be to make family life somewhat 'abnormal'.

AN ALTERED VIEW OF DISABILITY

A number of disabled writers[4,5,6] have suggested that disabled people, in going along with society's slavish devotion to 'passing as normal', have been agents of their own oppression.

Should disability be defined by how far a person measures up to normality, how easily they can do a task in the way that most other people would do it, the extent to which they look and sound like most other people and how much treatment, equipment or care is required to enable them to achieve the semblance of a 'normal' life?

The alternative view, and one that underpins the thinking of a cohesive movement of disabled writers, organisers, thinkers and artists,[7] is to see disability as a social experience, first and foremost, rather than a personal characteristic. Instead of focussing on physical incapacity, this view takes into account the impact of externals such as attitudes in the media, the accessibility of buildings, the extent to which disabled people, their families and friends are considered in the planning of most events and facilities and the limitations imposed by standard employment practice upon the working lives of disabled people.[8,9]

Looking at my own situation from this perspective, I asked myself not just how it feels to be a disabled mother but also what causes me to be a disabled mother in the first place. Is it simply that at a certain stage of my life I discovered that I have multiple sclerosis and over time the illness has reduced my ability to walk and limited the amount of energy available to me? Are other factors involved, such as the fact that so many of the buildings and facilities intended for family use are inaccessible to wheelchair users, or that the work schedules of most employers, which tend in any case to discriminate against mothers with young children, are even more of a barrier to me as a disabled mother?

Is the constant and unremitting assumption that anyone with a long-term illness automatically becomes a 'sufferer', a 'victim', a 'tragic case' or, of course, a 'heroine' or a 'battler against the odds', in itself disabling in that it devalues, marginalises and makes my experience seem abnormal in the eyes of others and possibly also in my own eyes?

This thinking about disability helped to shed light on the fact that so many of the interviewees expressed the desire to be seen as 'normal' parents. In a society in which so much store is set by being *normal*, there is a strong pull upon disabled and non-disabled alike to pass as such. Being a parent enshrines, perhaps more than any other social role, the right to participate in mainstream life. It is an initiating role, an active and adult role. To be disabled and a parent counters the assumptions of emotional dependence and passivity which are often made about disabled people.

Having demonstrated their right and determination to be a part of the mainstream of family life – sometimes, as we shall see, in the face of doubt and disapproval – disabled parents may be reluctant to draw attention to themselves. Perhaps it is not altogether surprising that many disabled people have inclined towards the imagery of normality and that some have felt wary, initially, either of identifying as disabled parents themselves or of making contact with others in a similar situation.

The lack of opportunities for contact with other disabled parents can result in people thinking that their situation is more exceptional than it actually is and lead them to believe that they are safer merging into the mainstream than standing out as being different.

With one or two exceptions, the disabled parents I interviewed could not be described as activists. A few belonged to charitable organisations such as the MS Society or Spastics Society (now known as Scope) and only one or two were members of organisations run by disabled people themselves.

Up to this point, as I have explained, I had myself tended to shy away from contact with other disabled people. Once I started on this piece of research, however, I discovered that far from wanting to distance myself, I found the contact with other disabled parents stimulating, on the whole enjoyable, often heartening, and always informative.

The Group
Portrait

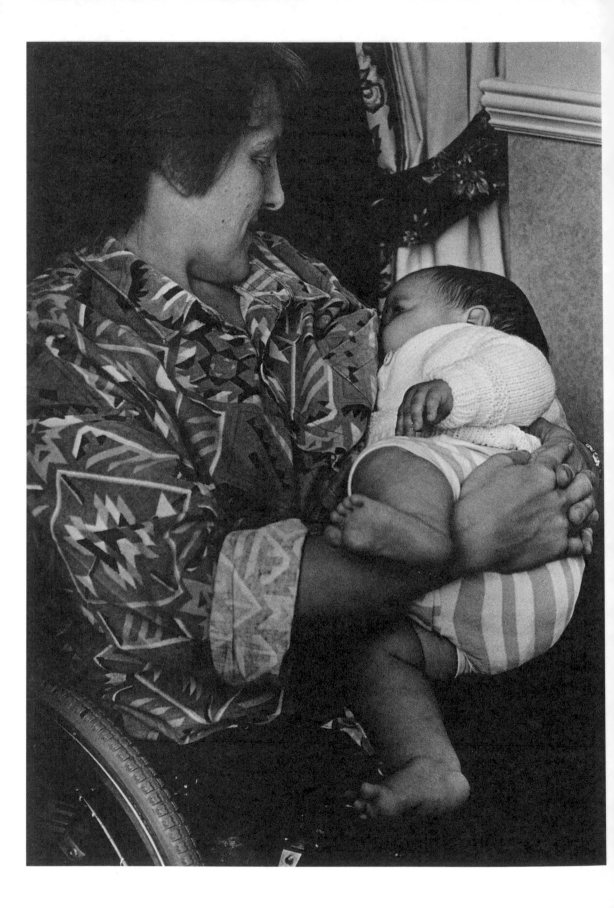

CHAPTER TWO

The Parents

The first part of this book is based on 21 interviews with 22 disabled parents. All of them had physical conditions that affected their mobility. Of the interviews, 18 were with mothers, two with fathers and one with a married couple who were sharing the primary care of their daughter. I chose this group for simple reasons – their physical situation had similarities with mine; their children were young like my own; we all lived within a radius of 50 miles. I was thus able not only to do what I hoped would be a useful piece of research but also to make contact with my peers and potential allies.

Alongside the common features of our experience there were significant variations, as can be seen from the biographical information summarised at the end of this chapter. To be raised as a disabled person is not the same experience as becoming disabled as an adult. To lose the ability to walk gradually is different from losing it overnight. People with conditions that cannot be seen find that they are treated differently from those whose disabilities are more obvious. The more an individual's speech and appearance differ from that of the majority of people, the stronger the reaction of strangers may be. Some of those I spoke to had stable conditions, others changed from time to time and some had progressive illnesses.

I did not have a large pool of disabled parents from which to choose a representative sample – I interviewed all the parents I was able to contact over an 18-month period which turned out to be overwhelmingly more women than men. It could be argued that since men and women face such different realities as parents it did not make sense to include in the study the few men I had spoken with. My own feeling was that I did not want to leave their insights out of the book. However, I have tried to indicate which observations apply specifically to the mothers I interviewed, those that apply only to the fathers, and those that concern both the women and the men.

I was struck by the fact that, although the circumstances were different in each case, all three of the fathers I spoke to had been at home sharing in childcare rather than out at work during the first years of their children's lives. It would be interesting to explore whether for a range of reasons, disabled men may be more likely to be involved in the primary care of their young children than their non-disabled counterparts.

I tried to give people the opportunity to talk about what was currently uppermost in their minds and explore issues that were of particular interest to them; I was less concerned about covering all aspects of the prepared list of questions. Many of those I spoke with had, like myself, limited energy and so it was important not to go on talking for too long. There were also practical matters such as school-day routines, babies' rest times, and so on, to take into account. My approach was aimed at giving people a chance to go into depth in their responses without having to continue the interview at too great a length.

In addition to its practicality, a strength of this approach was that it encouraged people to say most about the issues they had given the most thought to. I found that one or more key concerns emerged out of each interview which others would touch upon subsequently. In the following five chapters I have drawn out the main themes and issues.

For some, this was the first opportunity they had ever had to speak with another disabled parent; for one or two, the interview was their first evidence that other disabled parents even existed. Whether people were feeling satisfied with their experience of parenting when we spoke or whether they were finding things difficult, generally speaking our meetings were marked by a sense of solidarity and mutual pleasure in the contact. I was both a participant in and an observer of the discussions. I first tried out the questions I wanted to use by getting a friend to put them to me and note down my answers. Some of my responses are included along with those of the other interviewees.

Below I have summarised biographical details and the main concerns highlighted in each discussion. Unless the interviewee requested otherwise, I have changed people's names.

Sally

Sally separated from her husband shortly after her diagnosis of multiple sclerosis, leaving her to bring up their two daughters, aged six and nine at the time of the interview, on her own. She was walking with a stick and had limited use of one of her hands. She was working freelance as an academic. She spoke of the frustrations, for herself and the children, of having a progressive condition and of having to cope alone. She also spoke of the importance of support from the exceptionally close-knit urban neighbourhood she lives in and from her local church.

Jan

Jan has a condition which results in involuntary movements of her head, arms and hands. She has two children, aged two and four at the time of the interview. She is an experienced psychodrama counsellor. She talked about appearance and self-image; the fear of teasing and how this can turn out to be quite different from the reality.

Alison

After being diagnosed as having multiple sclerosis, Alison went on to have two children, a boy and a girl, who were five and three at the time of the interview. She had been a secondary school teacher but was now working part-time in community education. Her illness was in remission, though still affecting her energy level. She was interested in how disabled parents discuss illness and disability with their children.

Mary and Sam

Mary and Sam both had polio as children and met at a training college for disabled people. Mary uses a wheelchair all the time, whilst Sam uses one occasionally and otherwise walks with sticks. He used to be an administrator in a social services department but gave up work when their second daughter was born. Getting hold of resources that would enable them to live independently in the way that best suited their family was the major theme. Their older daughter was aged 12 and their younger daughter 19 months at the time of the interview.

Rachel

Rachel was a nurse but had to give up working when multiple sclerosis developed. She could walk only a short distance with a stick and over longer distances used a wheelchair. She had three children, aged between ten and four at the time of the interview. Isolation and the loss of opportunities to contribute were uppermost in her mind, along with constraints upon the lives of her children.

Annette

Annette was born with a condition which affects her legs, back and the use of her hands. It took some years for Annette's condition to be diagnosed. Although it is hereditary, it may or may not be passed on to her children. Annette walks with a stick on level ground and uses a manual wheelchair for longer distances. Her daughter was six at the time of the interview. Annette's determination to 'live as normal a life as possible' meant, for her, managing with the minimum of external intervention.

Beth

Beth developed multiple sclerosis when she was a young woman. At that point she had to give up her work with horses. Later, she had to leave a job in which she supervised the work of 120 women, because the travelling became too much. She worked up until shortly before her son, aged two at the time of the interview, was born, but had been unable to go back to work since then because her condition had worsened. She was assisting her husband with the business side of his farmwork but felt a sense of loss at not being able to develop her own career.

Kate

Kate has cerebral palsy and attended a special school for disabled children. She married her husband, who is also disabled, though to a lesser extent, whilst still at university. They both write technical books. They have two sons, who were 12 and nine at the time of the interview. Kate spoke about the effect of being raised disabled upon her development as a young woman and the challenge of parenting against the background of other people's misgivings and, at times, prejudices.

Liz

As an army wife Liz has lived in many places. She has spina bifida and finds both walking and climbing stairs difficult. She and her husband have three children, aged 17, 13 and nine at the time of the interview. She was conscious of the difference it can make to a disabled parent whether their environment is accessible or not.

Julie

Julie had recently had an operation on her hip which had been dislocated from birth but which had begun to give her pain. She had a baby of four months and two other children, aged four and seven at the time of the interview. Since the operation she could walk only very slowly with a stick and was unable to bend down or lift anything heavy. She hoped this state of affairs would be temporary but it was impossible to know for certain. She described the struggle to get hold of the resources the family needed, including the wait to be rehoused in a bungalow by the council.

Chris

Chris first had symptoms of multiple sclerosis as a teenager but had only been diagnosed a few years previously. Up until recently she had had a very active lifestyle, based around her home and garden. Since a multiple sclerosis attack two years earlier her energy had been very limited and she had been using a wheelchair. Her husband is a long-distance lorry driver and her three sons were 14, nine and eight at the time of the interview. She was very conscious of the isolation that resulted from not being able to get out of her home very often and the ways in which this affected her sense of herself as a person.

Helen

Helen has multiple sclerosis and walks with a stick. Fatigue, which is unpredictable, makes it hard to plan and so she is unable to do paid work. Her husband, a physiologist, has a very pragmatic approach to the effects of the illness. They find the village community in which they live supportive. Their sons were six and nine at the time of the interview. Helen felt well supported, though she spoke of the challenge of accepting other people's help at times.

Paula

Paula has a condition which affects her joints and so she has walked with sticks since childhood. She went to a school for disabled children from the age of 12. Her husband is a carpenter. The early days of parenting were something of a nightmare in which they were thrown very much onto their own resources. At the time of the interview their son was five and things were becoming much easier. Ironically, at this point they began to learn of some of the resources that could have been made available to them earlier.

Keith

Keith lost both legs in an accident. This happened a few years before he and his wife decided to start a family. He took three years off paid work around the time his first child was born. He has found being a father a rich experience and feels that, if anything, being disabled has helped in this. He talked about the way in which disabled parents can find themselves 'sidelined'. His children were aged eight and three at the time of the interview.

Joanne

Joanne worked until her daughter, now a teenager, was born. She was diagnosed as having multiple sclerosis when her daughter was three and so she and her husband left a gap of ten years before having their second child, aged six at the time of the interview. She currently uses a powered wheelchair inside and a scooter out of doors, which has enabled her to maintain her interest in a variety of adult education classes and in helping out at the local school. She and her husband are skilful in finding out what resources are available. However, Joanne was feeling deeply frustrated at the effects of her progressive illness and the inaccessible environment.

Tim

In the course of his work Tim received a head injury. He has made a slow recovery though he has not been able to resume his work. His wife works in the media and Tim is based at home with their 18-month-old daughter. He has assistance in looking after her. He felt that becoming a parent had been his most positive experience since the accident.

Karen

Karen is married to an American serviceman. She had been diagnosed as having multiple sclerosis five years previously, at which point her eldest daughter was three and she had twins of 11 months. Her illness follows a pattern of remissions and attacks and she has found it very difficult to get help at the times when she most needs it. Some of her neighbours have difficulty understanding a condition that is not always evident and this makes it difficult for Karen to set up the level of help she needs to cope with further attacks.

Shirley

Shirley left school at 15 and worked for a year in a factory, until she became paralysed as a result of a car accident. She lived at home until her first marriage at 22 which broke down after seven years, leaving her with a young son. A couple of years later she married Andy, a decorator, who has two sons by a previous marriage. Their own son was four years old at the time of the interview and Shirley's older son was nine. Her story illustrates how the attitudes of those around a disabled person play a part in the extent to which they are able to join in with activities.

Annie

Annie has cerebral palsy and was born in the north of the country. She went to a secondary school and, briefly, a college for disabled people. Her sons from her first marriage, aged eight and six at the time of the interview, live with their father. Annie was expecting a baby with her new partner, also disabled, whose two sons live with their mother. Annie was forceful on the subject of the prejudice sometimes shown towards mothers and pregnant women with speech difficulties and/or a different appearance.

Marion

Marion has a condition which makes it painful to walk, drive or stand for any length of time. Her husband is frequently away on business and at these times Marion is thrown very much on her own resources in looking after their children who were aged four and four months at the time of the interview. She talked about the issue of reciprocity. As a self-contained individual she would only ask really close friends for help.

CHAPTER THREE

Decisions Around Childbearing

PRECONCEPTIONS

'At boarding school they plan out what you're capable of before you even know it yourself. I've achieved more than they ever thought I would . . . Life is a process of learning – of doing more and more things for the first time.'

Mary

Eight of the parents I spoke to had been raised as disabled children. Those who had been to 'special' schools and training colleges felt that the expectations held out for them had generally been limited and certainly did not extend to parenting. 'At my boarding school they didn't expect me to learn to cook for myself, let alone raise a family,' said Mary. Kate, who attended a co-educational boarding school for disabled children said, 'We were given sex education, but no-one ever really talked about having children . . . I had siblings many years younger than me but somehow I never actually got to hold a baby until my own son was born, although the opportunity could so easily have been there'.

When they became pregnant these women found that the silence surrounding the subject of childbirth was replaced by anxious questions, often from members of their own families. 'Are you sure you'll be able to cope?', 'Have you considered an abortion?'. For the most part such reactions were discouraging, though Jan drew strength from a comment made by her mother.

'Just before I got married she said, "If you get pregnant and you can't cope, you could always have an abortion." She's very religious and it was a big deal for her to say that. I found it very liberating'.

Annie found that having successfully looked after one baby was no safeguard against the questioning of her decision to have a second. 'My mother-in-law said, "You've got one, isn't that enough for you?".' Sometimes complete strangers ventured an opinion. Liz, in hospital for the birth of her third child, was told bluntly by the woman in the next bed, 'You must be cracked going in for a third'.

Significantly, the most negative reactions were reported, not by the women whose practical abilities were most curtailed by their condition, but by those whose speech and appearance differed most markedly from the norm. Whether or not people recognise it, gut prejudice often plays a bigger role in determining reactions than rational concern.

Annie feels strongly that one of the areas in which prejudice towards people with disabilities manifests itself most strongly is around sex and child-bearing. 'People think that because you're disabled you don't do that sort of thing.' She recalls an incident when a friend's health visitor, 'asked me how we "did it"'. Annie replied, 'I jump off the wardrobe, what do you think?' and enjoyed watching the woman's confusion. 'You have to use sarcasm sometimes on people. Otherwise they just don't understand.'

When she became pregnant, a youth worker she knows suggested that after the baby was born she should bring it in to show the young people. Annie suggested that it would be even more useful to go in whilst she was pregnant, 'It might help them to make the connection'.

It seemed that those who became disabled as adults or in late adolescence had not met with the same expressions of doubt. For some it was regarded as a bonus. Keith, who had come close to dying in an accident joked, 'Having survived it seemed a good idea to capitalise by having children'. Shirley, paralysed whilst still a teenager, learned that the doctors saw no reason why she should not become a mother. 'After I'd realised I wouldn't be able to walk again it was a real encouragement to me and my parents to know that I would still be able to have children.' When she later became pregnant however, Shirley encountered incredulity as well as encouragement. 'I did get, "Should paras have children?" That kind of thing,' from some health professionals, including staff at the local hospital. The reaction from people around, such as neighbours, was more one of disbelief, "*Can* you have children?"'

The dialogue between parents and professionals

Health professionals and others who wade in with questions like 'Now have you thought this through?'; 'How will you cope?'; 'Have you thought about being sterilised?', should bear in mind the sheer volume of messages of doubt, anxiety and incredulity from those around and in the media to which disabled parents and prospective parents are exposed. This is an issue facing any health or social work professional who discusses childbearing and parenting with disabled people. A sense of antagonism can develop, not through any actual conflict of interests but because of a failure to recognise that there are sensitive issues of communication to be taken into account.

Annie recounted two incidents in which she had to struggle to assert herself in the face of assumptions being made about her. Her first pregnancy spanned a hot summer and one day when she was out shopping she started to feel very faint. Someone saw her hand shaking and called an ambulance, thinking that she was having an epileptic fit. As she lay on a hospital bed in casualty she overheard a nurse, who clearly disapproved of the fact that she was pregnant, say, 'Her doctor should never have allowed her to get into this condition'. Annie shouted from behind the curtains, 'The doctor didn't have a right lot to do with it'. The doctor who examined her maintained that she had had a fit. 'He didn't seem to know anything about CP.' Annie explained that she had seen plenty of seizures and was quite certain she had not had one. She pointed out that if she had had a Grand Mal she would still only just be coming round. Eventually she was taken home but the nurse's parting shot to the ambulance crew was, 'The doctor says she's had a possible Grand Mal but she's denying it'.

The second incident, or series of incidents, occurred when she had a miscarriage. At ten weeks she started bleeding and so she admitted herself to hospital. When she went for a scan the doctor said, 'Are you sure you were pregnant? If there was a baby it's not there now'. Then he walked out of the room. 'The way I was treated made me feel extremely angry. I had questions I needed to ask: Would I need a D&C? How long should we wait before another pregnancy? What form of contraception should we use in the meantime? The doctor didn't seem to want to answer any of my questions. Most of the other medical staff were the same. Trying to talk to them was like pulling teeth!'

None of the women who had multiple sclerosis mentioned meeting initial resistance towards the idea of having children. In a number of cases, though, these women and others were advised by medical personnel not to have a second or third child. Three mothers found the medical arguments persuasive and accepted this advice. For two of the three this involved terminating a pregnancy. Liz's consultant, who failed to persuade her not to have a third child, used the somewhat unscientific argument, 'You got away with two. Don't tempt fate by having a third'.

Some felt that medical personnel acted as though the fact that a parent or prospective parent was disabled gave them the right to ask impertinent questions or make pronouncements about the way couples chose to conduct their reproductive life. The opinions offered often felt undermining to the disabled parent.

Julie had gone ahead with an unplanned third pregnancy because she found the idea of a termination unacceptable. She felt that she had been 'ticked off' for this. 'The specialist who had operated on me got very upset with me when I told him I was pregnant. He said there was no point me even seeing him again until after the birth'.

Liz mentioned to her doctor that her husband was planning to have a vasectomy after the birth, as their family would be complete. The doctor urged that she should be sterilised because her partner was 'still a healthy young man'. She said, 'I went into this surgery feeling happy and pregnant. I came out feeling I'd be lucky to survive the birth'. Both Liz's husband and Helen's, who received similar advice, opted to have vasectomies on the grounds that it would be a relatively straightforward procedure for them compared to sterilisation for their wives.

The majority of people I spoke to said that they had decided to limit the size of their family, and in many cases the reasons given related to their impairment, most commonly the fear that their health might suffer as a result or the feeling that it would make it significantly harder for them to manage on a practical level. Several couples had deliberately left a sizeable gap (ranging from four to ten years) between pregnancies because they felt that this would be easier under the circumstances. Joanne and her partner had ended up with an even larger gap than they had anticipated because of poor health.

Several women felt that their physical condition had deteriorated as a result of childbearing. For a few women this had happened as a direct result of pregnancy and/or childbirth but for others it was less clear, since a condition such as multiple sclerosis might have worsened in any case. Either way, the long haul of broken nights and the physical and emotional exhaustion were felt by many to have taken a physical toll. Some felt that in the long term they would probably recover the lost strength but others were not sure that they would.

All the mothers in this situation made a point of saying that they would not want to be without any of their children, but some felt that they might have decided differently if they could have foreseen the consequences. One mother worried about the effect of this on her relationship with her son: 'How do you deal with the knowledge that a child's very existence has made your health worse? I'm afraid that one day when I lose my temper I'll let something slip'.

Helen and Karen had both been given a belated diagnosis of multiple sclerosis, and both felt that had they had access to more information at an earlier stage it might have made a difference to their thinking. 'Had the possibility of it being MS been mentioned after the first set of tests we might either have stuck at one child or left a larger gap. As things are, I wouldn't be without any of them, but I feel angry that we weren't given all the facts and trusted to make our own decisions on that basis. Some specialists seem to like to play at being God.'

THE PARENTS' DECISION

Even when all the information is available, it has to be recognised that ultimately parents have to make their own decisions. Marion, who felt that on the basis of her previous experience having a second baby might well cause her condition to worsen, decided to go ahead anyway because she felt it was so important for her first child to have a sibling. 'Nobody shares your childhood with you like a sibling does. When you're grown up it still goes on being important. I think about how important it is to me to have my sister as an aunt for my children and how my sister and I supported each other when my father died. You don't know the future and you can't legislate for it, but I wouldn't want to deprive them of the possibilities.'

Doctors told Annette that the effect of pregnancy and childbirth on her would be uncertain. In any case, her condition is likely to worsen as she gets older. This knowledge and the physical difficulties Annette had around the pregnancy and birth of their first child have made her and her partner very cautious about having another. 'All the same I feel that if I were to become pregnant again we'd go ahead, even if it meant my husband giving up work and staying at home to help. We'd dearly love to have another.'

For a number of would-be parents, finding out whether their

condition might be passed on to their children was a part of the process of decision making. Those whose condition could not be inherited generally found this reassuring but where there was a chance of the condition being passed on to a child or a grandchild, some individuals still felt confident about going ahead and having a family. 'I knew there was a chance of the children inheriting the condition, but I never let myself get into a state over it. I'd planned to have them and I was prepared to cope with the consequences.'

The speaker, Liz, who has spina bifida, was indeed aware of the possible consequences – a cousin of hers had had a baby with spina bifida that died. Since she was opposed to abortion on religious grounds, her choice was either to accept these consequences or to forgo having children altogether.

Some professionals have expressed disapproval of disabled people for taking the view that they are prepared to have children who could inherit their impairments but a different point of view can be put forward. Any parent may find that they have a disabled child – someone who themselves has experience of dealing with the practical and emotional issues involved and does not have to overcome disabling prejudices in order to accept the child in the first place, might in fact be better placed to cope than a non-disabled parent. Jan, whose condition was not genetically linked, expressed this. 'In my first pregnancy one of my fears, like most mothers, was that there would be "something wrong" with my baby. Second time round these fears lessened. Though I wouldn't wish it on anyone I knew I'd be well equipped emotionally. It would be allying.' These issues are explored further in a fascinating personal account by Anne Finger (1988) in her book *Past Due*.

Childbearing is not so much a once and for all decision as a series of decisions and revisions made over the course of a reproductive life – whether to have a child in the first place; whether to increase the size of the family and if so by how many; what size gap to leave between siblings; whether to terminate or continue with an unplanned pregnancy. Even when a decision is taken not to have any more children, other questions remain, such as what form of contraception to use, whether to opt for sterilisation or vasectomy. Although, *perhaps in part because*, there is a chance that they will be accused of irresponsibility, it was clear that this group of parents had given even more thought than most to such questions. There were also reminders that however much consideration is given, in the end fate plays a major role.

'When we got married we agreed that we would like to have children if possible. There was a lot of discussion and thought about how it would be. Consultants gave the all-clear to Mary and she felt she would be able to cope. It was an exciting time. We still dithered about whether to go ahead but the decision was finally taken out of our hands when Mary became pregnant. In fact the timing was pretty awkward because we had just moved into a flat which needed adapting, though looking back, it seems like just the right time.' There was a second, unplanned, pregnancy when their first child was four years old. 'We felt a bit panicky, especially as we were living in a fifth floor flat at the time but we decided to cope.' In fact that pregnancy miscarried at 11 weeks. Ten years later they took the decision to have another child – something Mary had always hoped to do. 'It was a difficult decision because we weren't sure that the big gap would work. In many ways it has proved difficult for Hannah; being a teenager, she has mixed feelings at times about having a toddler around.' Sam and Mary hope that in the long term the gap will become less important and that it will 'have been good for her character to have a younger sibling'. They feel that the family is now complete and they would not want to have another child.

A number of the parents said that disability had not figured in their thinking about whether to have children. For some this was because when the decision was taken the impairment either did not exist or affected them less. However, for a parent with a severe and obvious impairment to say that disability 'didn't come into it' can also be a way of asserting the right to be a parent; a counter to the tension between the parent's belief that they are doing something both natural and positive and the view communicated by others around them that they are doing something unusual or problematic.

Both for those raised disabled and those who become disabled subsequently, the decision to have a child tended to be seen in a very positive light. Annette's confidence in herself as a mother was clear; her eyes shone as she talked about her parenting. 'Disability makes no difference to loving and children know that.' Shirley said, 'The thing that gives me the greatest satisfaction in life is the fact of having actually had the children. I know several other "para" mums. We all feel strongly that our right to have children and a normal family life should be recognised and accepted. We're trying to be everyday parents, getting on with the job and coping with what we've got'.

CHAPTER FOUR

The Children

TEASING: FEARS AND REALITIES

> *'The greatest emotional block when I was thinking about having children was the fear of entering the world of children and having them taking the piss. All those memories of my own childhood . . . It hasn't been a problem at all so far but still you worry about your own children being teased.'*
>
> Jan

Because I talked with parents and not their children, the material in this chapter is based on disabled parents' perceptions of their children's situation.[1] As Jan reminds us, these perceptions are frequently based upon the speaker's own experience as a child. Disabled parents raise their children, and have themselves been brought up, in a society which is generally speaking dismissive of the rights and needs of disabled people and frequently belittling of them as individuals.

Those who grew up disabled had found themselves as young people from time to time on the receiving end of playground insults such as 'cripple' or 'spastic'. Those who had not been disabled as children, although they may never have used such terms themselves, had heard them being thrown at others and understood well enough the view they represented.

Eight parents mentioned a concern about teasing and it is significant that six of these were among the eight who were raised disabled. Their own childhood experiences heightened their concern for their children. Annie said, 'I'm not bothered on my own account about the possibility of the children being teased. I know I'm just their mum. All the same I am concerned for them having to handle it if they are given stick'.

Beth, who has multiple sclerosis, worried that her son would be 'taunted for having a mother who's not quite right'. Others expressed the fear that if their children were teased they might 'come to feel ashamed' of their parents as a result. Over time, a number of parents observed, their fears were not borne out by what happened in practice. 'We used to worry about the children being teased at school. We thought maybe they wouldn't feel free to bring friends to the house but so far there's been no real problem . . . It causes interest as much as anything'.

Of the actual instances of teasing that were given, several had been directed at the parent, though this had naturally also affected the children witnessing it. 'My daughter asked me not to bring my shooting stick down to school anymore because boys from the secondary school shouted out rude comments as we walked past.'

Several parents, because they had found it more practical to use reins or pushchairs beyond the customary age, had been on the receiving end of thoughtless jibes from onlookers: 'I used a pushchair much longer than I might otherwise have done, partly to stop him running off and partly because it made walking easier. That didn't stop some people, usually men, from saying things like, "Does he still like to ride in his pushchair then?"'.

The only report of children themselves being teased was related by Liz – an army wife. Two of her three children had had to contend with it. 'The children have had to go through teasing at times. My eldest son took less notice. If pushed too far he's liable to thump them. My daughter felt it more, though she's over it now. It hurts you, especially when you're the cause.'

Kate linked the attitude of children at her son's school towards her with the attitude of the teachers. 'I offered to do disability awareness work, but they didn't want to know. The teachers have problems with it themselves, if the truth be

'I don't think we need disability awareness training in this school.
We already support lots of charities.'

known. I went into school to help with art classes in the hopes that everyone would get used to having me around. It only really worked for the immediate group of children I was working with. One boy came up behind me in the corridor and called out, "Can you hear me?", assuming I was deaf. My son was very sensitive about it, so when he started his new school I made a conscious decision to play it the other way, and I never go in.'

Such a negative experience in school was fortunately rare, although by coincidence another woman I spoke to had children at the same school and she also commented on the negative attitude of the staff. A number of parents mentioned that they went into their children's schools to help. They found this useful, as Kate had felt it could be, in enabling them to form relationships with their children's peers and teachers.

Annie, whose sons live with their father, had had little opportunity to go in to their school. Shortly before we spoke she had been in to do some work on disability. Her sons seemed to take pride in her 'teacher' status and in their own knowledge of the subject.

When my own son started middle school I assumed he would be wanting to assert his independence by making his own way home. However, for the first term at least he asked me to come down to the school to meet him on my scooter. Often he would jump on the back and hitch a ride home. I was pleased to realise that far from feeling embarrassed about me being disabled he was actually keen to show off the scooter. At the same time it was a very natural way for his new friends and teachers to get to know me.

Chris, whose sons' school was inaccessible, nonetheless had a lot of contact with her sons' friends within the home: 'The younger boys constantly bring their friends round. They all sit in the sitting room, talking about anything and everything. I sit with them and throw in the odd comment. They take the wheelchair for granted. They don't give a damn about it'. Her next comment indicates that, although the wheelchair may not be as invisible as all that, the boys regard her warmly. 'When I transfer from an armchair back to my wheelchair, I am aware

42

that all eyes are on me. I can't help feeling embarrassed, but the interest is friendly. If my slipper falls off I'll just say, "Someone put my slipper back on for me".'

TALKING WITH CHILDREN

'I can talk ever so sensibly about the facts of my illness, but dealing with the emotionally awkward corners is altogether more difficult.'

Alison

Discussing illness and disability with children can take even the most open of parents into areas where they feel uncomfortable. 'I talk about anything and everything with the children – they knew the facts of life at the age of two – but we don't talk about my illness. I know it's to do with my own anxiety.' Another mother said that she found it hard to discuss her condition with her children because of its progressive nature. 'It's raw for me. I'm continually having to come to terms with it myself.'

Tensions sometimes exist between a parent's intention to be honest and candid and the desire to be seen in a certain way by their children. As Alison put it, 'I'm aware that I wanted my children to see me as being big, strong and dependable, especially when they were little. I don't want them to see me as second rate or inadequate, although of course I realise, that's not the right way to look at disability'.

The gap between the approach a parent adopts in theory and what might happen in practice was also illustrated by Annie. 'The best way to respond to children's questions is to be open. There's no point trying to shut them up. Let children ask embarrassing questions and answer them as best as you can.' However, on one occasion her younger son asked her: Why do you talk funny? 'I have no way of knowing whether he was referring to my speech impediment or the fact that I'm losing my northern accent.' Her answer to him was simply: 'because I do'. 'In the end I say what I feel like saying on the day.'

43

Frequently disability gets discussed in response to a child's question. 'My oldest asked me, "Will I get MS?" which was a good opportunity for me to talk about the illness but the twins haven't asked me any questions about it yet.' Individual children choose to handle the issue differently. Chris said of her sons, 'When I was first diagnosed the oldest asked me loads of questions. In the end I think he knew more about MS than I did! The younger ones seldom mention it. But they have their friends round here all the time and Peter very rarely brings anyone home'.

Some parents had come up with strategies to give their children a chance to talk things over, even where they did not feel able to talk directly about their own situation. 'I have a friend who has MS but the effects on her are much more obvious. This gave me an opportunity to discuss the illness with the children. It was easier to talk about it in relation to someone else.' Others had found it helpful to involve relatives and even professional counsellors in giving their children a chance to talk through the facts and air their feelings. Two women with multiple sclerosis had used a booklet written for children whose parents have the illness.[2] In both cases they asked grandparents to read the booklet with the young people.

Alison found that she was tempted to focus on the positive side – 'putting the attention on the things that can be done, rather than on things that can no longer be done'. At the same time she wondered whether this way of coping 'actually makes things harder in some ways for children – I sometimes wonder if it gets in the way of their being able to express difficulties and worries which the situation brings up for them'.

The approach taken by different parents in relation to talking to children about disability varied widely. Rachel and her husband made a point of talking things over with their children: 'We have discussed the illness very freely with the children from the beginning. They know I won't get any better. I feel they need to be aware of my limitations'. Liz and her husband encouraged their daughter to think about the implications for her own future. 'We encouraged her to do a study of the hereditary aspect of spina bifida for her GCSE.'

Annette's family preferred not to deal with the subject directly. 'We tend not to discuss disability with Samantha. When she's older it will come up in relation to marriage and having children, because of the hereditary factor.' Within the family there seemed to be a tacit agreement. 'Samantha understands about disability. She knows there's no difference between the disabled and the able-bodied. She gets angry if other children take the mickey. If I should fall over, Samantha simply goes for the cotton wool. She knows I'm all right. She accepts the situation. If other children happen to be around she'll tell them that her mother is ok.' Annette considers that she had the same attitude towards her own father, who walked with sticks. 'I accepted it without difficulty.'

Childrens' attitudes towards disability are shaped and constrained by the parents' own views and approaches. In one family, the subject of disability might be disregarded as far as possible, and seldom, if ever, talked about because the parents feel that this is the best way to assert the 'normality' of their experience as a family. Another family might choose to find ways to talk about disability, even where it feels awkward, because maintaining the ability to respond to whatever is happening is essential to the family's sense of itself. 'It pleases me if we can work through strong feelings together.'

Sometimes it is not possible to deal with something right away but there is a long term confidence in the family's ability to deal with the issues. 'I saw a programme about a mother who was very disabled and being looked after by her children. That's not something I want to have to look at with them at the moment. It's not something I want to think about myself. It's like looking at your own death. My kids might have to deal with those issues at some point but as long as the warmth and happiness are there, they'll be able to cope. I just have to hope that the right support systems will be there for them at the time.'

Many of those I spoke to felt that having a disabled parent gave a child the best possible chance of growing up with a well-informed attitude towards disability. Many parents saw this as being especially valuable in a society which generally speaking

45

offers little scope for children to discuss disability and illness. The opportunities that do exist are generally limited to seeing disabled people as a focus for fundraising efforts. Whether the concerns it raised were expressed or unexpressed, straightforward or complex, disability was a part of family life. Disabled parents are able to offer their children and their childrens' friends something unique; the opportunity to learn about the meaning of disability in the context of close human relationships, rather than through the mesh of society's ignorance and prejudice.

LITTLE HELPERS?

'If there's a specific task I'll ask the children to help, but generally I've arranged my life so that I can cope.'
Kate

Media concern about the subject of disabled people as parents has centred largely around the issue of children as carers and helpers.[3] Although severe cases of under-resourcing, where children supply long hours of assistance and perform tasks inappropriate to their age and strength, give cause for concern, it is important to realise that such cases occur when support systems have broken down. Many disabled parents find it objectionable that the media presents these stories as the norm and frequently lays the blame on the parents themselves.

A number of the parents I spoke to made comments in passing about being helped by their children, but it was not a major concern for any of them at this point. It is worth remembering that every parent, disabled or not, faces this issue in one way or another, though of course a disabled parent, dealing on a daily basis with the complexities of balancing independence, dependence and interdependence, can be expected to have given more thought to it than most.

Frequently the resourcefulness of parents and children came together to meet the practical requirements of the situation.

Rachel took pride in the fact that whilst she could no longer sew buttons back on, she had been able to train her children to do it for themselves. Shirley trained her young son to run his own bath, putting the cold water in first and then bringing her bath water in a cup so that she could test the heat. With both her sons she had been struck by their adaptability and the ways in which they had developed strategies at a young age to make it easier for her to give them what they needed. 'The older one used to stand by the wheelchair and crook his elbow, ready to be picked up. He was very light so I could lift him quite easily . . . In these kinds of circumstances children learn independence at a younger age.'

Paula's young son was large and heavy, which presented problems for her as she could not carry weights. However, 'from a baby Jack has had a sense of what to do. He never wandered off, and helped in various ways. He sorted out quite a few problems himself – at a very early age he learnt to pull himself upright. When I took him out on shopping trips he would do things like strapping himself into the car, pass me my crutches or carry the shopping in'.

These accounts of adaptability and helpfulness were balanced by accounts of non-co-operation, sometimes from the same children. 'Samantha helps hang out the washing and helps with the shopping. All the same she has her defiant moments when she'll run off out of reach.' Even Jack, who had generally been so 'uncomplaining and helpful' had his moment of defiance. 'On one occasion he threw a tantrum when we were out for a walk and lay down on the ground demanding to be carried. I had to wait for half an hour, conscious of everyone looking, until he was prepared to move on.'

Whether children were helpful or not was seen by parents to have as much to do with their personalities as with the parent's approach and situation. A mother with multiple sclerosis said, 'Everyone told me that children of disabled parents don't run off. It's not true. My son was a runner, pure and simple; the fact that I couldn't chase after him only added to his fun!' Another mother said, 'The oldest is naturally good and helpful and this rubs off on the younger one. They know their mother can't pick their toys up and they know they have to do it themselves. We expect them to be responsible but we're careful not to depend on them'.

A carefulness around getting children to help was mentioned by others also, 'I feel that it is important that my children can choose whether they help me or not. If I ask one of them to get something for me and they go and get it, that's great. If they say no I accept that too, even if it does leave me in a fix. I don't want them to feel that I can't manage without their help'.

'The girls aren't a lot of help to me – they're too selfish, which is only what you'd expect for their age. I don't keep on at them to do this, do that, and I accept any help they do offer and then praise them and sometimes try to explain why I appreciate it so much. Perhaps that will have a more long term effect on their willingness to help than if I continually bitch and moan . . . I'll let you know if it works – in ten years time!'

One mother found that she had to change her approach when it became clear that her young son resented her requests for help: 'When he was four he started to say "No". Now I tend not to ask them to help me. It's increased my general wariness about being over-dependent'.

'THE THINGS THEY GAIN ARE MORE IMPORTANT'

> '*It's a toss-up at the end of the day whether you think the children gain or lose out from having a disabled parent. But I think that the things they gain are more important than the things they lose.*'
>
> Sam

Several parents said that there were things about living with a disabled parent or parents that their children clearly enjoyed: 'The children love it when we all play together on the bed, playing cards or having a rough and tumble. They like to swing on the monkey pole pulley.' 'Their friends really like my scooter. I think they find it easier to talk to me because I'm on the same level.'

A number commented on, and clearly valued, the fact that they spend a good deal of time sitting down with children engaged in a shared activity such as reading, playing a game or just talking. 'I'm aware that I spend more time sitting down with the children reading and playing than I might otherwise have done. They enjoy that.'; 'There isn't the same temptation to be rushing about and getting things done . . . also, you come to value the things you *can* easily do together.' There was a strong sense of the value of these times, which were seen to bring emotional and educational benefits. Paula always found that she spent a lot of time doing things together with Jack, 'reading, making things. The teachers say he's very intelligent so I suppose all that attention must have had a good effect'.

Keith noticed that he is 'extremely patient' with his own and other people's children: 'I'm happy to let them do things at their own pace, however slow that may be. It suits children to move slowly because it's more their pace'.

For some, there was a strong awareness of the things that could *not* be done together. This was particularly painful where children themselves expressed a sense of loss and deprivation by saying things like, 'Why don't we go out so often any more?' Sally felt that a child who has grown up with a certain reality tends to accept it, whereas a child who remembers a time when the parent was more mobile may experience a sense of loss. 'The older one remembers how it was before, when I could drive, and so it was easier for us to get out and about. The younger one doesn't have those memories.'

It can also work the other way, so that changes in the parent's situation are seen as positive by the child. Chris, who had recently started to use a wheelchair in the house as well as outside, was surprised by her son's reaction. 'One day he came home from school and found me standing in the kitchen. He said, "What are you doing walking about?" I said, "You didn't think I was going to spend the rest of my life in the wheelchair did you?" He said, "At least when you're in the wheelchair you don't get bad tempered and you don't get cold".'

Two or three parents felt that they had started out with a tendency to try to compensate for the fact that they were disabled by taking their children out whenever possible or by making sure they did not miss out on any of the activities their peers were involved in or simply by giving them more attention in the home. 'If anything, I may have tried to over-compensate. Second time round we've had a more relaxed approach.'

Some interviewees expressed an awareness that their children might on occasion be exposed to physical risk because they could not always physically intervene between the child and danger. 'Mobility is always a worry with young children. Even if your child doesn't wander off you worry that they might because you know you couldn't catch them.' Nevertheless, these same parents and others spoke of how their children had become independent at an earlier age than children with non-disabled parents and were thus better equipped to deal with potential hazards. Some reported a greater concern about safety because they would feel 'so unbearably guilty if anything were to happen'. Others felt that they were more relaxed, philosophical even, because of their physical limitations: 'You can't make it any safer by worrying'.

Sometimes choices have to be made that involve an element of risk. This is probably true for all parents, but may be more apparent for the disabled parent of a young child. The risk may not always be physical in nature. A woman with multiple sclerosis sometimes took her preschooler to outpatients' physiotherapy with her. Although she felt good about showing him a positive aspect of the hospital's work, she was also concerned that he might see something in the course of one of their hospital visits that he found upsetting. 'On balance it's worth the risk. If something came up we could always talk about it.'

My own children from time to time reckon up the tally of gain and loss. 'There are some places we can't go with you, but when we go to a theme park we don't have to queue up for the rides. It's a pity you can't play running games but we like it when you can't catch us when we're naughty! It's horrible when you fall over but it's fun playing with the scooter.' My daughter, who is still just small enough to ride on my lap in the wheelchair, has always enjoyed how easy this makes it for us to talk to each other and also enjoys the positive contact with strangers. 'Wherever we go you need help and so we're always meeting friendly people.'

With older children, there were other concerns. From the parents I spoke to with children of secondary school age, I learned that three out of these seven older children had received or were receiving child guidance. This is a high proportion. Should it be seen as evidence that children of disabled parents are more likely to have emotional problems? It should be borne in mind that young people whose parents have continuous contact with health and social services are more likely to come to the attention of service personnel. By the same token, this group of parents may be better informed than the general population about the range of services which are available. Also, in part because of their sense of responsibility, they may be less inclined than non-disabled parents to let things ride or to deny the existence of problems. One mother commented, 'All parents should have access to advice without the taint of behaviour problems'.

Some parents reported that they had been on the receiving end of criticism and harsh words from their children. Although this could be extremely discouraging and painful, it did not necessarily undermine the parents' confidence that they were doing a good job. 'The children won't see it because it's just a part of their lives, but I like to think I'm a good role model. I don't give up when there are problems.'

CHAPTER FIVE

Self-Image

DISABILITY AND SELF-IMAGE

'I imagine a scene where I'm sitting with the children out of the wheelchair, feeling very normal. We enjoy playing all together on the bed, playing cards, having a rough and tumble. The children like to swing on the monkey pole pulley. Those are some of my happiest times – I feel free.'

Shirley

Several of the people I spoke to made a point of telling me they did not think of themselves as 'disabled'. This did not seem to be related either to the extent of the individual's impairment or to the length of time that they had been affected by it. It was more that their view of themselves did not sit comfortably with their feelings about the way in which disabled people are regarded. Annette, for example, said that she has never considered herself to be disabled and 'likes to be treated as an able-bodied person'.

Others had grappled with similar issues around the way they see themselves and had come to different conclusions. 'I no longer feel bothered about being disabled, but I do resent the limit on the things that can be done and the consequent boredom at times', said Shirley. She was very conscious of the constraints on disabled people but had come to see them as reflecting society's limitations rather than her own. 'I'm more prepared to fight for things these days. But it shouldn't be necessary to battle all the time for things that I have a right to.'

Annie's story illustrates how someone who had no difficulty

in speaking of herself as disabled and identifying with other disabled people, still balked at having to deal with the image disability has in the eyes of others, to the extent that she was prepared to live apart from her sons. 'The children's father was prepared to fight the battle for custody but I was not. I didn't want my disability being used against me and discussed in negative terms around the boys. I just want them to see me as their mum.' It was ironic that Annie, who elsewhere in the interview identified herself as a 'very maternal woman' felt that she had to let go of the day-to-day rights of mothering in order to ensure that her sons should see her as their mother first and foremost. Her sons have continued to live with their father in the north of the country and Annie sees them during the holidays. She feels that she is only just beginning to come to terms with the guilt of having left them. 'Mothers don't leave their children.'

Annie, who has cerebral palsy and is a veteran of a school and college for disabled people, described what she saw as 'the pecking order' in disability – she felt that both disabled and non-disabled people have a tendency to rank different impairments in a kind of hierarchy which is often implicit but rarely stated. 'When I'm out with my friend who's in a wheelchair people automatically address me rather than her. Then they discover that I've got a speech impediment and after that they don't know where to look or who to speak to!' Annie's own son unconsciously picked up on the idea that some impairments are more acceptable than others. 'He took me on one side and said, "It's alright. I've sorted it out at school about your disability. I told them you were in a car accident!".'

A similar idea has been discussed by Vic Finkelstein (Senior Lecturer, Department of Health and Social Welfare, Open University) who points out that groups of disabled people sometimes attempt to guard their own sense of acceptability by distancing themselves from 'groups that they perceive as more disabled than themselves'.[1] It was perhaps a reflection of societal prejudice, internalised within disabled people themselves, that a number of women said that they had been offended at the assumption of a link between physical impairment and learning difficulties. 'If your body doesn't work properly people can't accept that your brain does', and, 'People talk over my head. They think you're blind, deaf and daft'. The struggle to weaken other people's assumptions – 'the more you try to show your intelligence the more certain people resist what you are saying' – drives a wedge between two groups of parents who in fact experience similar prejudices.[2]

Towards the end of each interview I invited whoever I was talking with to imagine that a photographer, spending the day with them and their families, could capture moments of their family life, at its most rewarding on the one hand and at its most difficult on the other. My intention was to get a direct feeling for the experience of the individual; literally a picture of it. The exercise appealed to most people and produced graphic cameos of how people saw themselves and their family life.

The responses brought very clearly into focus a theme which recurred throughout the interviews, namely the importance of being seen as a 'normal' parent, a 'normal' family. I was struck by the number of times the idea of normality was invoked as people described the positive scenes they would want a photographer to capture. 'We're doing the things normal families do', 'We're all together doing something ordinary'. 'A good scene would be sitting with the children out of the wheelchair, feeling very normal'.

I said earlier in the book that the importance that most parents in the group attached to the concept of normality took me by surprise. After all, my starting point had been to ask myself why disabled parents make particularly good parents and in what ways is their experience *distinctive*, rather than how far it either conforms to or departs from the norm.

Talking about normality is, amongst other things, an assertion of the everyday nature of family life. Disabled parents' lives are taken up with the same basic tasks as other parents:

feeding children, getting them off to school, going shopping, dealing with tantrums and all the rest. Disabled or not, life has an inescapably familiar quality and every family's way of doing things is normal to them – no matter that a bed-hoist might seem alien to you, in this family it is a piece of everyday equipment and a much loved toy.

Some of the responses given illustrate the play that can exist between the sense of normality and the sense of difference. Shirley celebrates the normality of playing with one's children whilst at the same time relishing what is distinctive about the experience for her as a disabled mother. Annie also chose a scene suggesting both 'normal' and 'different': 'A positive image would be sitting around playing a game or reading, the normal things. The children are very used to being around disability; they have no problem with wheelchairs. I'd rope my friend Jackie in for the photo session – she's a wheelchair user'.

In another example, the 'normality' of family life challenges onlookers' assumptions about the 'normal' experience of the wheelchair user: 'Sometimes when we're out we really muck about with the wheelchair. Me and the children are loaded on and my husband careers along with us; zigzagging, heading towards bushes and turning at the very last moment. We're all shrieking and people are watching open-mouthed. It's not what they expect someone in a wheelchair to be doing. I enjoy having fun as a family and I also enjoy the sense of confounding people's expectations'.

Sometimes it proves possible to confound one's own negative expectations too: 'I find photographs painful, videos terribly so. I feel that I look ugly and bizarre. Just a few photographs have contradicted that. I really didn't want any pictures taken at our wedding but actually they turned out very well. I have a perception of a family portrait of these three lovely looking people and me standing out. Actually it's the perception rather than the reality. Phil took some wonderful pictures when we were on holiday. Many I can be proud of. Group pictures give me the sense that I'm included – that I'm just different'.

FEELING RESPONSIBLE

'One of the other mothers was trying to coerce me into joining in with the parents' race (at a school sports' day). In the end I just told her bluntly, "I've got MS". Then I felt guilty because she was shocked and embarrassed.'

Karen

Several women reported thoughtless jokes or comments, often tossed off to relieve the speakers' awkwardness or embarrassment, that remain a hurtful memory for those on the receiving end. 'It gets wearing being the butt of people's jokes day after day,' said Karen. Rachel, however, had found a straightforward way of dealing with comments. 'When people see me walking they sometimes think I'm drunk. My response is to be completely straight with them and tell them what the problem is. Then the ball's in their court.'

Other people's perceptions and projections in some cases directly influence the disabled person's lifestyle. It was pointed out in the introduction that we live in a society that tends to view disability as a personal characteristic, first and foremost, rather than a social experience. One result of this is that it is easy for both disabled and non-disabled people to assume that it is part of the disabled person's role to take responsibility for the reactions of family, friends and even acquaintances for difficulties which arise out of the experience of being disabled.

The interviews, and in particular the observations made by the women I spoke to, bore this out. Karen, quoted above, who has three young children, was at risk of having a further attack of multiple sclerosis if she became overtired. Nonetheless she gave up her social services care assistant when she was feeling comparatively well because neighbours had indicated that they did not think she was ill enough to justify receiving the help. 'Do I have to wear a label round my neck saying DISABLED?' she wondered.

Paula too, felt hurt by her neighbours' assumptions. 'People tend to talk round here. They look on from a distance, draw the wrong conclusions and say thoughtless things.' Paula keeps her house spotlessly clean and tidy. 'They assume I'm getting help or that John must be doing the work. They say things like, "Poor man, he'll be needing his holiday!" I bite my tongue so I don't get worked up. It makes me feel guilty.' John tells her to ignore the comments. 'People can't imagine how I've managed with Jack. I dread to think how they think I've brought him up.' Perhaps it is partly in response to external criticisms that Paula feels she is 'very wary of putting too much on John. I would rather push myself than keep asking him for help'.

Feeling responsible for the situation was often accompanied by an impulse to protect family members and friends from negative feelings. 'I try not to get emotional in front of the children . . . I don't like to burden my own parents with my problems.' One woman said that she was afraid that if she talked too much about her problems she would come to be seen as burdensome by friends. Two women with progressive conditions indicated that, if it came to it, they would rather go into residential care than become too great a burden on their families. 'It might be easier for everyone not to have me around. I wouldn't like to think it would come to that but if it would enable the family to get on with their lives I wouldn't make a fuss.'

Many of the women interviewed described the strategies they used to contain painful feelings: 'When I feel bad I prefer to shut off and go to sleep until I'm feeling better.' 'Generally my response would be to try and keep it within myself and try to cope with it. I'd try to talk myself out of it and remember that others are worse off.' Some felt that this was a practical necessity to enable them to keep going. 'I'm on my own such a lot I couldn't possibly give in to self-pity – I'd go under with it. I've got to keep myself busy'; 'I have my moments but I tend to keep them to myself. If somebody showed me sympathy when I was feeling bad I'd just dissolve. I prefer to do my dissolving by myself'.

'People can't imagine how you cope.'

Physical and emotional isolation are to an extent imposed by circumstances – not being able to get out to work, limited access to the places where people meet, the inaccessibility of public transport – but on occasion it is self-imposed in order not to drive people further off by being seen as needy or burdensome. Ironically, this concern about other people's feelings, which led so many of the women I spoke with not to disclose difficulties, is the very behaviour likely to be interpreted as heroic.

In many ways women found it as uncomfortable to be regarded as heroines as they did to be subjected to negative assumptions. In either case, it felt as though they represented something for the speaker that had little or nothing to do with who they really were. 'People, sometimes complete strangers in the street and sometimes people you've known for years, come up to you and say, "Aren't you marvellous!", or "I'd never be able to cope as well as you do". I suppose they mean to be encouraging, but it has the opposite effect on me. It's quite hard to explain why. It feels as though the speaker is putting a distance between my life and theirs.'

Several women mentioned being on the receiving end of comments like those in the quote above. In each case it was described as an unwelcome experience, all the harder to deal with because the speaker believes that they are paying a compliment. Chris said forcefully, 'I get very tired of hearing, "Aren't you marvellous", "However do you cope?" or "I do think you're brave". On one occasion I just flipped, "Do I have a choice? What do I do – go to pieces or go to hell!" You cope because you have to'.

Choosing to contain emotional needs is clearly not the same thing as having no emotional needs in the first place and to some this feels a necessary and yet vulnerable route to take. 'Self-pity just makes me miserable,' said Chris, 'you just have to come to terms with it.'

Six interviewees mentioned the significance of the emotional support they had received from counselling-type resources. Being able to work on issues arising from their situation with people other than those immediately involved was valued. Two people had used interactive forms of counselling (Re-evaluation Counselling, which is a form of reciprocal counselling, and Psychodrama respectively), which had the advantage as one woman put it that, 'they involve giving out as well as taking in, which feels very self-respecting'.

Increasingly, when children receive educational child guidance their parents are also offered counselling. The four parents I spoke to in this situation all said that, whether or not the counselling had proved useful to the young person, they personally had found it helpful. 'We felt guilty; we couldn't help thinking that perhaps the reason she was having problems was because we are disabled. The counselling helped us deal with that.'

RELATIONSHIPS WITH PARTNERS

> 'Actually, it's impossible for my husband to get it
> right – if he offers to help I don't like it. If he doesn't
> help I get annoyed!'
>
> Paula

All of those interviewed, apart from Sally, who was divorced and living alone with her children, were in long-term heterosexual relationships of between three and 18 years standing. Two women had children by earlier marriages and they both had step-children too. In every case partners topped the list of those offering practical support, and generally speaking they were noted for their helpfulness. Emotionally, however, the picture was often more complicated. It has already been stated that, even with family members, many of the interviewees were reluctant to air negative feelings about their situation, and in many cases this included partners. A full disclosure of feelings was seen by some as putting yet another burden on their partners. Some suspected that their spouses were themselves struggling to deal with feelings of pity and helplessness. 'I know he'd love to be able to make me better ...

we were out shopping and I saw him looking wistfully at another couple as he was getting the wheelchair out of the car for me. I knew he was thinking, "That's what it used to be like for us." I felt really bad for him.'

In a number of cases, the impression I received of the interviewee's relationship with their partner was of a situation of fundamental goodwill, overlaid with unconfirmed conjecture about how the other might be feeling, wistfulness and unresolved emotions. Mixed feelings and a degree of ambivalence are a feature of many, if not all, close relationships, and are by no means confined to those in which one partner is disabled. Nevertheless, when a partner is disabled, the presence of such emotions can make it harder to accept the partner's practical assistance. Some interviewees said that they had turned down offers of help, either because they feared their partner was expected to do too much and might become resentful, or because their partner's over-solicitous attitude made them feel uneasy in some way.

In several cases non-disabled partners had made changes in their working lives, whether temporarily or permanently, in order to fit in better with needs at home. These changes included giving up work altogether (in the case of Sam who is himself disabled, though to a lesser extent than his wife), changing working hours, changing to another type of work, getting a job closer to home and going self-employed. On the whole such changes were welcomed by the disabled partner, though sometimes the feelings were mixed. Chris, who felt that the home was very much her domain, confessed that having her husband around more, after he gave up his job as a long-distance lorry driver, had been difficult. 'It didn't really suit either of us. It was a relief when he went back to work.'

There were few interviews that did not touch at some point on tensions and stresses within the partnership and these were often seen as being linked or else exacerbated by the difficulty of living in inaccessible environments with inadequate practical support. Although John, a carpenter by trade, has always been helpful and supportive of Paula, the period after their son's birth put a lot of strain on both of them initially. 'We exhausted ourselves; every little problem seemed to be doubled.' Although the frustration and fatigue had receded as Jack grew older, Paula felt that the strain of that period affected them emotionally and physically.

Julie and her husband were driven to exhaustion by the combined stress of her post-operative mobility difficulties and the fact that his job as a postman started at 4am. 'Two weeks after I came out of hospital we had a huge row. Now he's a cabinet maker so the hours are better. If we weren't so close I think the stress of it all it could have done for our marriage.'

Karen and her husband are both very stoical and generally keep quiet about their feelings. 'He's very even about the whole thing, but he doesn't express sympathy. Sometimes it would be good if he did.' Yet when I asked her who she would talk to if she was feeling really low she said, 'My husband is the one I'd talk to. If he knew I was really upset about something, he'd be there'.

Alison, who generally found her partner supportive on the emotional level, nonetheless hesitated to rely too much on him in that respect, 'It's not always good to put the burden on those who love you. Relationships can grow lopsided'. On a practical level it was also helpful not to have to depend on him. She found having a social services home care assistant extremely beneficial in terms of its effect on their relationship. 'It sounds strange, but it's actually made me feel more independent having help. It's eased the tension that was always there between us about the untidy house. It gives us both room to breathe.'

Helen's account of her husband's approach to her illness stood out, not because he was necessarily more helpful than other partners, but because it seemed to her entirely unproblematic. 'He genuinely doesn't seem to regard it as a nuisance. He approaches it quite practically, looking always for the most effective way of doing things. He doesn't make a fuss and he doesn't seem to feel sorry for me either. He's not frightened by it . . . He tends not to proffer help but he always responds readily when I ask for it. It's comforting to have someone competent around. He fills the holes that I leave.'

ISOLATION AND SELF-IMAGE

'Neighbours are either out at work or occupied with small babies. I've always been sociable and I really miss people dropping in.'

Chris

A number of the parents I spoke to felt isolated as a result of not being able to go out to work – this was accentuated by the fact that many neighbours and friends do go out to work and are therefore not available during the day. Chris enjoyed interacting with her own children and their friends but she was clear that this did not replace the contact with other adults that she was missing, especially during the day when the children were at school. 'There's no-one here at the point when you need to discuss things . . . I don't feel that I am as strong-minded as I was. I'm strong-minded enough to keep going but not so able as I was to hold my own.'

Being focused on the home and valuing being available for children does not reduce the need for other interests and adult companionship. Because Shirley does not go out to work she spends more time with her children. 'In some ways it's very good. I love the fact that they can always bring their friends home. They can do that because I'm here, not out at work.' At the same time, actually being prohibited by the benefit system from going out to work, even part-time, is a cause of frustration to her because she finds she gets bored.

Joanne, in addition to her evident parenting skills, demonstrated a striking competence in getting hold of appropriate resources. Having test driven six scooters, she had been in a position to buy a second-hand one, confident that it would not only meet her requirements but also that she was getting a bargain. Nonetheless she too expressed a lack of confidence: 'I don't feel I have any achievements,' and she regretted the isolation of being stuck at home whilst most of the women living round about her were out at work.

Paula had little or no contact with other mothers when her

son was a baby and so 'any problems I had I put down to the fact I was disabled'. She recently realised, to her surprise, that a non-disabled neighbour was 'having more difficulty coping with her new baby than I ever had!'

For several of the women I spoke to, looking after home and family was vital to maintaining a positive sense of themselves and so this was a priority, however demanding it proved. Chris had been offered a home care assistant by social services but had declined. 'I've got no desire to sit and watch someone else do my work. However long it takes, it's my job organising the family and making the food . . . I just enjoy being able to do for them.' Joanne, who had formerly enjoyed a range of handicrafts, said that, with decreasing strength in her hands, 'I feel I need to keep what little mobility I have in my hands for cabbage and carrots'.

Others – often, though not always, those who had some form of further education – had different priorities. For these women, to be engaged in some form of work, whether paid or unpaid, was important for the maintenance of a positive self-image. They might find it easy enough to pass on household chores to others, so long as they had the opportunity to extend their role beyond the immediate family. In Kate's words: 'Working for a degree, far from being a burden, saved my sanity. It was something else to hang on to . . . I see it as a definite plus that I've always had some other project on the go'.

Rachel spoke of her sense of loss at no longer being able to work as a nurse. 'I keep my union membership up to date because of the psychological value of knowing that I could offer professional help in an emergency.' Beth too, deeply regretted not being able to return to the work she most enjoyed. Sam, who had given up full-time work in order to help more at home, continued to give a lot of thought to the dilemma of whether to go back to work or not. If he were to work part-time, the solution which would suit the family's situation best, he would lose his benefits without having enough to live on. 'All things being equal, it might be better psychologically if I was back in paid work. Having the situation practically under control is one thing but beyond that there's a need for a sense of purpose and direction which can come from paid employment. Going out to work imposes a sense of structure and routine which can be lacking otherwise.' Sam finds that calls for help arising out of his voluntary commitments 'sometimes come at very inconvenient moments for the family, which can be very awkward when you have young children'.

About half of the parents I spoke to expressed a desire to do part-time work or said that they were looking at the possibilities for doing some form of training or adult education class. Frequently however, they went on to explain what prevented them from doing this – the threat to benefits, the inaccessibility of classes, courses and potential workplaces, the inflexibility of working hours, the lack of money to buy necessary equipment and transport difficulties were all mentioned.

Where a disabled woman or man has been in paid employment before the arrival of children, and does not have easy physical or social access to the places where parents meet, the birth of a child may bring a sense of isolation greater than anything experienced before. Several of the women I spoke to felt that the experience of birth and early parenting had in fact caused their physical condition to worsen and that this had an additional effect on their chances of making contact with people outside the home.

Paula had visitors when her son was small, 'but I always felt they'd come to see the baby rather than me'. Her most regular visitor had been an aunt of her husband's who would come and take the baby out for walks. Although she appreciated the aunt's willingness to help and the fresh air and change of scene for the baby, the effect on her at times was to increase her sense of loneliness and exclusion. 'I wondered, "Does anyone really care?"'

One effect of the difficulty in getting out is to limit access to news about what is going on in a child's school – whilst some of it comes home in news bulletins and letters; other important information is pinned up on the notice board, or gleaned from a word dropped by the school secretary or a conversation at the collection point. Disabled mothers whose children get a lift to and from school miss out on all this. Some might argue that non-disabled mothers who go out to work have to deal with the same difficulty. They do however at least have the compensation of the companionship of other adults in another context. What many disabled mothers found hard was the double deprivation of being excluded from both the world of work and the world of informal exchanges between mothers.

CHANGES

'It's been a case of dragging myself up by my boot laces, but I've survived to learn and grow.'

Kate

A number of people touched on ways in which they felt they had changed as a result of the experience of parenting. Generally the changes were viewed in a positive light, particularly by women who had been raised disabled. Kate said, 'If you're a disabled person you're not really encouraged to grow up. Being a parent has definitely helped in that process. I'm a much more resourceful person. The more you're encouraged to do the more you can do'. She went on to describe how her expectations of herself as a parent had changed over time. 'At the outset I felt under pressure to try and be a supermum because it had been so difficult in the first place to convince people that I would be a competent mother. I couldn't admit to them or myself that I wasn't coping.' For her, the process of coming to terms with the realities of motherhood was very much tied in with the process of self acceptance.

Shirley felt her accident interfered with the process of growing up, 'I missed out on my teenage years, the rebellion, going your own way and all that. I was wrapped round my parents'. Looking back she feels that her first husband, 'didn't know what he was doing when he took me on; he couldn't cope at all. When we went out he would wheel me into a corner and leave me there, which I hated. He was trying to change me to

67

'Another inch and we'll be in.'

what I couldn't be and I was shy and frightened in those days'. Her second husband, Andy, has turned out to be really good with the children and 'great for me'. With the encouragement of him and his friends Shirley feels she has become much more outgoing. 'Nowadays I get to parties, dances, go for meals out – we've tackled all sorts of new things – ferries, aeroplanes, continental holidays.'

In Keith's view, 'becoming a father is often the thing that changes a man most'. In his case this transition more or less coincided with changes that occurred in his life as a result of his accident. Although this made it impossible to say exactly which changes were due to which causes, he felt that becoming disabled had forced him to become both more patient and more home-based and that both these developments had dovetailed with the demands of parenting. For his wife, however, he felt that having a disabled partner had 'almost certainly made mothering more difficult' because of the constraints it introduced in where they could go and what they could do as a family.

Three women commented that they had found themselves using their voices more forcefully as their physical mobility decreased. For Joanne this had proved embarrassing at times: 'Where another mother might move across the room to intervene in a fight over toys, I would use my voice, loudly. Everything would go strangely quiet!'

Julie found that she was developing a quieter style of parenting. 'Before the trouble with my legs flared up I used to shout and go bananas. Now I reason more, stay calm and appeal to their better natures. I know and they know that I wouldn't be able to get hold of them to smack them, so I have to keep the situation under control.' Whilst Julie was finding reasoning with her children useful, Kate revealed that reliance on the spoken word had proved a double-edged sword in relations with her sons, 'I've had to resort to psychological warfare at times. Now they're older they've learnt to turn that back on me'.

Becoming more assertive in dealings with the outside world was generally regarded as a virtue but it could also be problematic, depending on the circumstances and the individuals concerned. Forceful self-presentation might lead to a breakthrough in relations with one intimidating health professional but cause the relationship to deteriorate further with another.

It was typical of the women that I spoke to that they described themselves as independent and self-reliant. Pride was taken in this, but it was also felt that it could get in the way of asking for help when it was needed. Several women described how they had to override to some extent what they saw as the independent side of their characters in order to ask for help when it was needed. Helen said that she did not consider that her personality had fundamentally changed in this respect; 'I have simply had to learn to adapt my behaviour'.

It was perhaps not surprising that those whose physical condition was stable or improving tended to express more positive feelings than those who were dealing with the challenge of a worsening condition. Whatever the physical situation of the individual, however, the extent to which they felt *in control* largely determined the extent of their satisfaction with their experience of parenting. Whereas one mother might take pride in the fact that she felt she was providing her children with the same or possibly greater  opportunities than their peers, others stated their satisfaction in more limited terms; 'I say to myself that I've managed to stay on my feet another year', or, 'I take pleasure in anything that I can still do better than the children'.

CHAPTER SIX

Being on the Edge and Being Involved

PARTICIPATION

'A good scene from family life would be me sitting in the chair reading the Sunday paper after a proper Sunday lunch. The children are occupied with their own things at the table. We're all together and we're separate too . . . It's very peaceful. A bad scene might be similar on the surface but completely different in terms of how it feels: It's Sunday again. The table is covered with all sorts of stuff. The children are screaming because I promised them they could make a cake. There's mess everywhere and no energy to clear it up. My partner is emotionally absenting himself, saying "What does it all matter?"'

Alison

Both participation and non-participation have their positive and negative sides. 'Joining in' is not automatically a good thing, if it costs too much physical effort, for example, or if a person is made to feel unwelcome by others involved in the same activity. Non-participation, on the other hand, is not necessarily a bad thing, for example if someone chooses to withdraw in order to rest, or is able to opt out of a strenuous family activity and still feel involved in what is going on. This was illustrated by responses to my request for scenes to illustrate the highs and lows of family life. A moment in which the family is doing something 'all families do' might be given as a positive example because it suggests integration and normality, or as a negative one, because at that moment it is such a struggle to keep going.

Alison made this point by offering the same basic scene on two different occasions both to illustrate what she finds most rewarding and most frustrating about family life. Others also chose as their 'difficult' picture times when they were managing to carry on but had the feeling that things were getting on top of them. A scene chosen to represent what is satisfying about family life might still be demanding but with the disabled person feeling on top of things.

The scenes people chose to represent their difficult times as parents were in many cases the kind of hectic, impossibly demanding moments familiar to every parent. 'A difficult scene would be me trying to dish up dinner, the children all wanting drinks and there's someone at the door . . .' In each case, however, the presence of disability was seen as aggravating the demands of the situation, as in Sam's description of a harassing moment in family life: 'A bad time is between 4 and 6pm, before dinner. Every member of the family is trying to do something different. Hannah may have come home from school in a bad mood. Emma is playing up because she's hungry. I am trying to get out to a meeting. Mary is trying to get the meal or maybe needs twenty minutes to herself in the bathroom. We're all shouting at each other and I'm feeling split four ways'.

It is possible to be comfortable 'at the edge' and at the same time very uncomfortable 'in the thick of it'. A scene where the disabled parent was on the fringes of an activity was described by Rachel with a sense of loss, 'My little girl is on her swing at the bottom of the garden. I'd love to be able to push her but I can't walk that far so I'd be standing watching her from the back door'. Alternatively, being on the edge of things can feel like involvement at an appropriate level, as in Helen's account of herself with the family in the garden: 'I imagine myself sat on the patio under an umbrella whilst Simon and the boys look in the pond. They bring something over to show me. I'm a part of it and I'm involved but I'm also resting'.

Opting out of family activity can be welcome at times. Sam and Mary each valued having time to themselves. Sam: 'My time to be by myself is in the morning before everyone else gets up. There are no interruptions and I can really concentrate on whatever I'm doing'. Mary: 'My time is late at night after everyone's in bed. It's the only chance I get to be completely by myself'.

Sometimes feelings are mixed: 'Generally we do things together as a family. John says that if I cannot join in with an activity then he would rather not do it. Occasionally Jack and John do things together – a heavy job in the garden, or going out in a boat. I think it's good that they should do things together but even so it's impossible not to feel left out at times like those'.

Keith described how he has found himself marginalised on occasion in the presence of other adults. 'Finding yourself side-lined leads to a lack of control . . . Generally speaking I don't find there is much you can't do with young children from a wheelchair. It's not that there's a real problem for me in doing things; it's just slower and requires more effort.' The problem arises when other adults are present because they automatically move in. 'Either they imagine that things are actually more difficult than they are, or they're not sure what to do, or they feel it's holding things up.' Keith's way of dealing with this is to set up occasions, both with his own children and with nephews and nieces, when he's the only adult present. 'I'm quite confident that if there's no other adult around I'll be equal to whatever needs doing, even if it means I have to get out of the wheelchair and use my arms to get up a flight of steps. You can't not bother when you've got children to look after'.

The crucial thing is not how much a person joins in but how far they are in a position to determine the extent of their involvement and the form it takes, rather than having it dictated by external circumstances and other people's attitudes.

ACCESS

'We thought we'd try a new restaurant for a change. When the manager saw me in the wheelchair he said to Andy, "They usually phone first". Who exactly did he mean by "they"? We went back to our usual Chinese and were made welcome. All the same, it would be nice to be able to branch out a bit sometimes.'

Shirley

Access is not a clear-cut, once-and-for-all matter. A number of examples from the interviews can be used to illustrate this. A community centre, designed to be wheelchair accessible, became inaccessible since nobody knew where the key to the disabled toilet was. For a mother walking with sticks, a classroom that felt welcoming at the beginning of term became a nightmare to negotiate by the end of term as tables and chairs were moved around. A wheelchair user was invited to a mother and toddler group in an accessible venue, but the room was arranged in such a way that she could not supervise her child effectively and so she did not return.

On the other hand, a building that is officially inaccessible becomes accessible if there are enough willing and physically strong people around to help – although any wheelchair user who has been hoisted up a flight of stairs, however willing the lifters, will tell you that it is not their preferred mode of entry!

A shingle beach presents a natural rather than a man-made barrier to participation. But if a family with a disabled member goes to a shingle beach for the day, the difficulty that the disabled member has in joining in comes about as a result of a *social* decision, albeit one that the disabled parent may have helped to make.

Sometimes, accessible alternative routes are provided for parents which are socially isolating. 'At one of the schools I went to look around, the headmaster said I could use the back

entrance as it would be easier than the front. I didn't like the idea because I felt I wouldn't be able to get to know the other parents.'

Ill-informed attitudes can present a greater barrier than physical obstacles. As well as the unwelcoming reception the family met when they tried a new restaurant, Shirley described how she had been unable to see her sons' performance in the school play because she had been instructed to stay at the very back of a crowded school hall 'because of the fire risk', even though there were exits at both the front and back of the room.

Several parents reported that they could not get into their childrens' schools, whilst one mother had the deeply frustrating experience of a child who was at a wheelchair accessible school being assigned to the one upstairs classroom! 'It would be hard to say which of us, Jo or me, felt that we missed out the most. It was the school's loss too, because in previous years I'd always been in to help out in the classroom.'

Barriers to the parent's participation can result in the exclusion of the whole family, or in the loss of opportunities to do activities together which most families would take for granted. 'What I regret most is the loss of opportunities to do things spontaneously as a family', said Joanne. 'We can't just say, "it's a lovely day, let's go out for the afternoon". The whole trip has to be planned in advance and the route has to be mapped out around access and toilets. There's no way we could just take off and leave it to luck'. Not to be able to watch or hear a child doing something that she or he enjoys and wants to share is a great frustration for many disabled parents. 'Why do so many swimming pools and sports centres have upstairs viewing galleries?', Keith mused.

Five of the people I spoke to lived either in Milton Keynes or close enough to go shopping there. Living myself in an inaccessible city I was struck by their descriptions of the practical advantages. 'There's a purpose-built network of pathways which pedestrians, cyclists and wheelchair users can use to get around the town. It makes taking Emma out much more straightforward than it was when we were dealing with a child of the same age and living in London. It also means that Hannah can safely take her younger sister out for walks.' 'Where we live there are very few shops you can take a wheelchair into. I sit outside and send Samantha in with a note or, in some cases, the shopkeeper comes out to me. But in Milton Keynes it's really straightforward. I can get into all the shops.' Even so, I was told, the local access group has to be constantly vigilant against accessible buildings becoming inaccessible as a result of internal changes.

For many parents the greatest limitation on their family life was the lack of suitable transport. Two-thirds of the parents in my study were not able to drive and several of these had had to give up driving because of their impairments. Erstwhile drivers and people living in rural areas felt particularly keenly their subsequent reliance on the expensive taxi service or inaccessible public transport. Alison had found it a huge help having a disabled parking card. 'It can make a whole day much less stressful. Using car parks which are a long way from where you need to be is a strain for all parents but for me it can be the final straw. Being able to use the car maximises opportunities for doing things with the children – it breaks through the trapped, passive feeling you can have if you're confined to the house . . . Maybe they should rethink the wording on it though – it says, "this person has great difficulty in walking". That's not strictly true in my case, yet the sticker is indispensable.'

Quite a few of the people I spoke to either did not drive or did not have access to cars. Some were unable to use their cars because of the impossibility of getting a wheelchair in and out without assistance. Buses, for most families an essential form of transport, were not an option for most people. Liz found buses in England 'much more of a struggle' than in Germany where she had also lived.

Taxis for most families were too expensive for anything but occasional use. For getting out and about locally, some have access to a scooter or electric wheelchair but many either cannot afford such equipment or would feel uncomfortable about using it.

The issue of participation and non-participation, involvement and non-involvement, goes beyond the apparently simple question of whether a place or an activity is accessible or not into questions about social choices and priorities.

MUTUALITY

> 'A lot of people do swaps – looking after each others' children. I couldn't do that. I can look after my own two safely enough but I could never undertake to look after three or four children on my own. It wouldn't be safe.'
>
> Marion

When non-disabled parents help each other out, it is very often on a reciprocal basis. Sometimes this is made explicit in organised exchanges of child care and sometimes it is just a tacit understanding that favours will be returned as and when the opportunity arises. Several of the disabled mothers I spoke with raised the issue of reciprocity as a constraining factor in their lives.

Marion expressed the dilemma for her: 'Maybe there are other ways in which I could repay people but some people wouldn't be happy with that. In cases like that it's better not to fix anything up at all. We've never got involved in the local babysitting circle because repayment has to be in kind and we couldn't do it'.

Others had friends or neighbours who insisted favours did not need to be returned, but this could still be difficult to accept. Rachel had a friend living nearby with children of similar ages to her own. 'We often go to the park together and she's friendly and helpful but I'm wary of doing too much with her. If I'm in her house I can't do anything to help, make the tea or whatever.'

At the same time, Helen and others made the point that if the tables were reversed they would not hesitate to give assistance to a friend in their own situation. In what has been called the 'gift relationship'[1] it is easier to be on the giving than on the receiving end. Helen spoke of the helpfulness of her village neighbours. 'I don't like asking but if I do, I know they'll help. They'll be happy to, as I would too if it was the other way round. They'll ring to see if they can get anything from the shops. I don't like to rely on others but I have to come to terms with the fact that I have to.'

At Annette's daughter's school there is another mother who uses a wheelchair. Annette said that she would prefer to ask this woman for help than one of the other mothers. The fact that both women are wheelchair users creates a sense of parity. Also, perhaps, an unspoken understanding of when *not* to offer. 'Sometimes we help each other out, though even then it depends what it is. Mainly we prefer to get on by ourselves.'

The manner in which help is offered can make all the difference to whether or not it can be readily accepted. There is no formula for this, just a sense of ease. What makes one offer of help acceptable and another not is a very individual matter and has a lot to do with the level of trust between people. 'A good friend bullied me back onto my feet after the last MS attack. Her way is to pile in with help, possibly too quickly at times.' This friend however was very near to the top of Beth's list of allies, 'because I know how deeply she cares about me and my son'.

Over half the parents mentioned a friend or neighbour they could call upon to help in an emergency; someone who, 'could be contacted at any time of the day or night'. In some cases these individuals were viewed as a last resort or safety net who could be turned to in a real crisis. In other cases they were described in terms that suggested that the relationships had the intimacy, dependability and ease associated with good family relationships. In such cases, there exists the knowledge not only that someone could be called on at any time but for any reason – it would not necessarily have to be a crisis at all. I think of a good friend of my own who I feel I can ask for help at any time. If the situation is not an emergency and it happens not to be convenient she will always tell me, which is helpful because it means I feel free to ask. Reciprocity exists in these relationships, not in terms that can be quantified but in mutuality of feeling.

Two mothers mentioned friends of this type who had moved away, leaving a feeling of deep and ongoing loss. 'I hate asking for help, I absolutely loathe it. Having said that, it depends very much on who I'm asking. I had a friend living nearby that I felt I could ask for help at any time. Now if my husband's away and I run out of something I just have to wait till he gets back.'

HOUSING

'*When we moved I had a frustrating few months whilst the new home was being adapted. I felt as though I'd got worse but I hadn't really – it was because nothing was right in the house.*'

Mary

Mary's comment illustrates the relative nature of disability. A wheelchair user living in a bungalow adapted to her or his individual requirements is less disabled in terms of day-to-day living than a person whose impairment is less extensive, or even temporary, but whose house presents a series of practical obstacles. Even where an individual's condition remains constant, a move or other change in circumstances can throw things into disarray. A mother or father whose home is set up in such a way that they can do household chores without difficulty may find themselves in a dependent situation when they go away on holiday to an unadapted cottage or caravan.

Generally speaking it is easier to make practical plans around a stable condition than one which fluctuates or is progressive. I sometimes feel that I am caught in a limbo land between using a wheelchair and walking with sticks. This is awkward both practically and psychologically. Should the house be planned around the way things are today or the way they might be in a year's time? Today, going up the stairs once or twice a day is difficult but it is also valuable exercise. At any point, however, the stairs could become an insurmountable barrier. Becoming a full-time wheelchair user and moving house or adapting the home would seem sensible but it feels as though it would commit me to a course of action I am not yet wanting to take, that is, giving up on the limited walking ability I have. Amongst other things, that would make it more difficult in the long run to get into the houses of friends and relatives.

It can be hard to sort out in all this what is sound practical thinking and what is slavish adherence to 'carrying on normally', where this is actually inappropriate and may even get in the way of finding a workable solution. Since my partner and children are *not* disabled, whatever house we live in needs to work at wheelchair height and standing height too. Instead of feeling stalemated by my dual existence it makes sense to plan around it. Finding the resources is the next hurdle and, of course, facing the upheaval that domestic changes inevitably involve.

All the interviews except one were carried out in people's own homes. I was struck by how few of them were adapted to suit the physical needs of the interviewees. Although everyone I spoke to had an impairment or condition that affected their ability to walk, only five were living in bungalows, ground-floor flats or adapted houses. Four of these were full-time wheelchair users, though Joanne, a wheelchair user, was still living in an unadapted house. Two were couples in which both partners were disabled, but Annie and her disabled partner were living in a first-floor flat.

Those people who were unhappy about their housing situation tended to have given the matter a lot of thought. Several couples were thinking about moving to single-storey accommodation. Two families were on council waiting lists for a transfer. Those that owned their houses were in some ways faced with a more intractable problem. To buy a bungalow in the same area would tend to cost more and give less space, and, as Joanne pointed out, 'life with a wheelchair requires more space, not less'.

Joanne and her husband discovered that the council would pay a grant of several thousand pounds to put a wheelchair lift into their house but they would not be prepared to give any financial help to enable the family to buy a bungalow. 'In fact the house turned out to be unsuitable for a wheelchair lift, so we ended up with nothing. We could move to another area where bungalows are cheaper, but all my contacts are here, this is where I'm known. I would find it terribly hard to start all over again somewhere else.'

Often those living in bungalows had predominately elderly neighbours who in some cases made it clear that they did not welcome having a family with young children living nearby. Shirley commented, 'The neighbours tend to be elderly and a bit intolerant of children. It's hard on children when they're needing to make a noise and you have to keep telling them to be quiet'. Kate, whose husband was also disabled, said, 'When we moved in the neighbours were terrified. They thought we would need a lot of help. They've relaxed over the years somewhat. They're still not friends, but there's one or two who could be called on in an emergency'.

Mary and Sam, who lived in a bungalow in a new town, benefited from the enlightened policy of planners who made a point of including bungalows in areas of family housing because they recognised that some parents would be disabled. All the same, the move involved them in far-reaching changes. 'We came here from London chiefly because it gave us the chance to live in a bungalow, though at the time we knew nobody here.' The home needed extensive alterations and Sam gave up his job at that point, 'to get things organised in the house for Mary'.

Paula and John live in a house which presents considerable access problems – in addition to the stairs which are difficult for Paula it is up a fairly steep, 25-yard path along which handrails have been fitted. Parking is on a grass verge or across a busy road and up a lane – but for the time being they have decided against moving. 'John has lived all his life in this house. He bought it from the council when his parents died. Had he known at the time that he would marry me he might never have bought it, but as things stand we could never afford to buy a bungalow in this area and in any case, it would be a great wrench to leave this particular house.'

The thought of starting again in a new place can be even more daunting for a disabled person than it is for a non-disabled person. It is harder to meet new people because of poor access and, in addition, many non-disabled people respond awkwardly at first. 'Close friends don't have any difficulty in accepting my situation but others who don't know how you'll react approach cautiously or keep their distance.' The importance of knowing the physical layout of a place, which buildings are accessible and to what extent, which shopkeepers will come out of the shop to serve a disabled customer, where the dropped kerbs are, and so on, cannot be over-estimated.

Housing is a complex and often challenging issue for disabled parents, frequently fraught with difficulties to which there is no completely satisfactory solution. A central problem is that the pool of suitable private and council housing is minute, highly priced and generally inappropriately located. The situation would change radically if legislation required that all new housing be built with access in mind, as is already the case for public buildings.

This would have the advantage of enabling disabled parents to visit other people's homes, reducing the isolation that many experience. The greatest benefit of all would be that instead of disabled people having to make the best of accommodation that does not meet their practical needs in order to  be part of 'normal', family life, society as a whole would notice that what is in fact normal is that people are physically different from one another and that it benefits everyone if these differences are accommodated.

CHAPTER SEVEN

'You Shouldn't Have to Fight'

GETTING HOLD OF RESOURCES

'They're hopeless around here. I feel I've had to fight for every single thing.'

Julie

'I've found the services generally very helpful.'

Chris

By chance, I had the opportunity to interview two women, Julie and Chris, who were both living in council owned houses on the same estate in a country town. They had heard of each other's existence but had never actually met. Both women described themselves as, 'a prisoner in my own home'. Beyond this inescapable similarity, their experiences were strikingly different. When they spoke about local services it was hard to remember that they were actually living in the same place.

It is important to look in more detail at what these two women said. Their accounts highlight some of the factors that affect the distribution of resources to disabled parents. These include service providers' perceptions of the onset and likely prognosis of an individual's illness or condition and also their interpretation of the role of the wider family. Julie and Chris also show how an individual's feelings about disability can influence their practical course of action.

Two years before I spoke to her, Chris had a dramatic and medically high-profile flare-up of multiple sclerosis. Around that time, she started to use a wheelchair inside the house as well as outside. The attack prompted the local health service and social services to take a number of measures aimed at providing support for the family and to assist Chris in caring for her three school-aged sons.

Chris's family had applied for and been allocated a council house with an adapted ground-floor bedroom. She had been offered (though she had in fact declined) a social services home care assistant. The children were given transport to school, and when she visited the physiotherapist she was provided with transport in an ambulance. Her overall view was that the local services had been responsive to her needs, and she felt reasonably confident about the range of resources available. Her mobility was severely constrained, however, by the fact that she was having to wait for an electric wheelchair to become available on loan.

Julie was born with a dislocated hip that had not been diagnosed until she was two, following which she had two operations. It had never been more than a minor problem for her until a few years earlier when she began to be in a lot of pain. At that point she had a further operation. Technically it was said to have been a success and the doctors considered that she was recovering, albeit slowly. The birth of a third, unplanned, baby had made life extremely difficult. Julie and her family were experiencing this period as one of acute crisis and were aware of needing far more support than was currently available, especially since two of their three children were under five and the youngest still a baby. Julie could walk only with difficulty and was still in some pain.

Julie's perceptions of the local health and social services were almost the complete opposite of Chris's and she felt very poorly supported. Her social services home care assistant, for which, as she pointed out, she had paid the going rate (there is a fixed charge and she was only allocated two hours), had been taken away due to cuts in the service. The family was waiting to hear if they could be rehoused in a bungalow, but had been given no indication of how long this might take.

Meanwhile, Julie was struggling to get her small baby up and down stairs in what she felt were dangerous circumstances.

She had given up visiting the physiotherapist because she could not manage the walk and no transport had been made available. Although she had requested it, her school-aged child had been refused transport to school. The reason the authorities gave for this was that they felt the child's grandmother could walk him to school. She was in fact doing this already, but Julie felt that it was an imposition on her mother, who was also expected to be available to help her with her housework and childcare needs, although she was working part-time. Julie felt that the authorities were using the fact that both her own parents and her in-laws were living close by to 'let them off the hook . . . they tend to say "get them to do it"'.

Several women found, as Julie did, that having family members, and in particular the disabled person's blood relations, living close at hand could make it harder to get hold of resources. It was felt that social service departments work on the assumption that families will be both able and willing to step in with help. Similar assumptions would not be made about other sources of support within the community; for example, that a disabled parent who attended a church would automatically be provided with all the practical support they needed by their fellow church members or that someone living in a village or close-knit neighbourhood would have little need of external services. Yet in a number of cases people received more help from sources such as these than others did from their families.

Where there were aging parents, they were often not well placed to help in spite of their concern. 'My parents live opposite and are very helpful in spirit but they're too old and frail to do much practically. In any case I would object to having my own parents push my wheelchair. It wouldn't feel right.' Indeed, in some cases, elderly parents needed a certain amount of looking after themselves.

Paula, whose relationship with her mother and sister was so distant that she rarely saw them, even though they lived in the next village, was told by her GP after battling on for some years without assistance, '"We thought your mother was helping you". From that point of view it has been a positive disadvantage having family living locally.'

It is possible that in time, support would materialise for Julie as it had for Chris. Part of the problem, though, seemed to lie in the fact that Julie's situation was not regarded as a crisis. The operation had been a technical success, she was officially recovering, and she was deemed to have support from her extended family. In other words, according to health service and social services criteria, this was not an emergency requiring fast mobilisation of resources. Julie's common sense, however, told her that the family urgently needed more support. Her difficulties would, all being well, be temporary – but if she were to fall on the stairs whilst carrying the baby, the resulting damage could be permanent.

Even situations that, unlike Julie's, meet the criteria for immediate response, do not always attract resources in time, especially where the need is short-term. Karen, who also has multiple sclerosis, had a flare-up of symptoms which caused her difficulties in looking after her three children, including pre-school twins. 'By the time the promised help materialised, the attack had passed and the need wasn't so desperate . . . one of the problems in having a pattern of attacks is in knowing when to go for help and who to turn to in the first instance'.

Where a disease or disabling condition progresses gradually similar problems can arise, since there is no crisis to trigger service providers to assess needs or pass on information. To a certain extent, this was my own situation and it was only as a result of talking to other parents in the study that I first learnt about a number of resources I was entitled to.

In some cases, individuals who had been disabled since birth or childhood had less information about the resources available to them than those who had become disabled as adults. Once a person is seen as being able to manage their life independently they may have very little interaction with social and medical services. This may be a welcome relief to individuals who have had to struggle to set up a degree of independence in the first place, but it can also leave them short of appropriate information and resources to maintain that independence when circumstances change.

Paula and John struggled to cope when their son was small. 'Had we known what to ask for perhaps it would have been provided but we didn't know what was available and no one ever thought to tell us . . . In the last couple of months, now that the need is nothing like so great, social services has offered me a home-help. Recently I applied for Disability Living Allowance. My GP said, "I hadn't thought of that". When we asked the social worker to assess us for a chair lift she came to the house and made some other offers too. She said of several things that John had done, "Oh we could have done that for you". There's a sense that nobody's ever come forward with anything. It's all had to be pushed for and none of it was there when it was most desperately needed.'

Disabled parents and prospective parents need access to information, equipment and assistance that does not require a health or family crisis to mobilise it, but is available on the basis of current need. The NHS & Community Care Act of 1990 enshrines the principle of person-centred rather than service-led provision but this laudable aim often appears to be in conflict with the constraints of organisational practice.

THE CALL FOR GREATER FLEXIBILITY

'I feel there are enough restrictions on my life, as it is, without having to be in the house whenever the home-help is here.'

Joanne

A number of interviewees spoke of the lack of flexibility in statutory provision; the rules and regulations around the services of home care assistants were a particular cause of frustration. Several mothers were under the impression that assistants were not allowed to help with childcare. I am informed that if this has been identified as a need by a domiciliary services manager, time can be allocated, though the individual assistant would need to be police-checked first, which may be why some assistants said that they were 'not allowed'.

The organisational requirements work against a flexible response to the day-to-day demands of the mother's situation. People receiving help were required to be in the home for the duration of the visit and appointments could be cancelled or rearranged at very short notice. Although a number of mothers commented on how useful they found their home care assistants, it was a further frustration that they were given no choice about who came or for how long.

The provision of equipment was frequently hedged round with restrictions. When my son was at nursery school I asked the local social services department if I could borrow a large but lightweight collapsible buggy which I knew they kept in stock. The buggy, because of its size and stability, would have enabled me to get up the path to his nursery class. Without the equipment I was unable to manage the walk and so on bad days I was having to send my son up the path with one of the other parents, thereby missing out on contact with his teachers and on the experience of seeing him in his classroom. I was informed that the rule was that the buggies should be issued only to the parents of disabled children and the rule, it seemed, could not be broken. It made no sense for me to invest in such an expensive piece of equipment for a few months use and so I had to do without, all the time knowing that a suitable buggy was sitting in the store room at the social services department.

Tim, who was at home during the day helping to look after his small daughter, encountered a similar inflexibility when he asked the occupational therapist if a hand rail could be fitted on his stairs; 'I was told it wouldn't be possible because my condition was improving'.

Remember Rachel, unable to go down the garden to watch her daughter play? This is a further illustration of the fact that definitions and labels, rather than actual needs, often

determine the access to resources. According to grant-making criteria, an occupational therapist told me, it is not considered essential for a disabled parent to be able to get to the bottom of their garden, 'unless of course, the child is designated hyperactive'. Once again the allocation is defined in relation to the child without the situation of the disabled parent being taken into account. In practice, as with the example of the pushchair, it is both the parent and the child who lose out as a result of this inflexibility.

One of the reasons such rigid rules exist is that they are a means of rationing resources in a climate of cutbacks and increasing constraint upon public spending. Health service personnel frequently claim to be frustrated about having their hands tied in the allocation of resources. Whilst acknowledging this, it is important to point out that inflexible regulations based upon fixed definitions discriminate unfairly against people who do not neatly fit the assumptions underlying the provision of services. Disabled parents are more likely than most *not* to slot into pre-defined categories because as disabled people they are not expected to be caring for others and as parents they are not expected to be physically impaired.

Mary and Sam felt strongly about the way that inflexible support from their social service department and the rigidities of the benefit system in effect combined to dictate the family's lifestyle. 'We are very aware of the need for change in the whole set-up. We don't want or need constant help – we want to have times on our own. What's needed is more flexible help, available at times which suit every member of the family.' They feel that an ideal solution would be to have direct control of the money social services uses to assist them so that they could make their own arrangements and they were planning to discuss the options with their social worker.

There is also 'the vexed question' of whether Sam should return to work or not. Full-time work would impose too many pressures on family life, in particular the need to find suitable help for Mary 'which would only work if the system was a good deal more flexible than at present'.

Disabled parents are the people best placed to decide how much and in what form assistance is required at any given time and to fit this into the overall picture of family life. In some places social service departments have carried through with the logic of this thinking and after a shared process of needs assessment are putting cash into the hands of disabled clients to buy in their own assistance.[1]

Mary and Sam's vision has, for some disabled parents, become a reality and looks set to do so for many more, as a result of the Direct Payments Bill which is under consideration by parliament at the time of writing. Enabling people to employ their own personal assistants has been shown to be cost effective,[2] but the changed way of working may involve social workers in a shift of power and the challenge to professional assumptions needs to be acknowledged. Concern about the *shortage* of resources may be used, unconsciously at times, to mask underlying issues around the *control* of resources.

LIMITING OR LIBERATING?

The point has already been made that access has social and psychological dimensions as well as physical. Limitations on participation are not dictated purely, or even largely, by the degree of physical impairment, but also by such factors as physical and social access, the attitudes of others, and the personal perceptions of the disabled person about the degree to which a piece of equipment or a particular offer of help is psychologically acceptable.

In this respect too, the differences between Chris and Julie were illuminating. Chris said how much easier her life had become since she had taken to using a wheelchair. 'I think back with horror, really, to an occasion a couple of years ago when I was out with the family on an outing, struggling to walk fast enough to keep up with everyone, though the whole thing had become a nightmare. Some people think using a wheelchair is the end of the world. But for me it's been an enormous help. I sometimes think, "Thank God I'm in the wheelchair".'

The fact of being defined as 'disabled' was not an issue for Chris at this time. What interested her was to attain the best quality of life within her limitations. Julie on the other hand, having discovered that an operation intended to relieve pain had in fact drastically reduced her mobility without significantly reducing her pain, was dismayed at her present degree of impairment and was for the moment quite opposed to the idea of using a wheelchair. For her it would have represented 'giving in' and so, as she saw it, would have made it harder for her to work towards recovery.

Their different attitudes towards using wheelchairs would have made a more significant difference in the lives of the two women had it enabled Chris to get out and about independently whilst Julie was confined to her home. The fact is that the estate they lived on was too steep for a manual wheelchair to be used independently and Chris could not afford to buy an electric wheelchair and so both women were effectively stuck at home whilst their husbands were at work. In the evenings and at weekends when their husbands were around, however, Chris was able to get out of the house, whereas Julie was not because she did not want to be seen using a wheelchair. Then again Chris could only go to places that were accessible to wheelchairs, which, as it happened, did not include her children's school.

As well as dealing with the practicalities of the situation, disabled people also have to deal with other people's attitudes and their own preconceptions. If you have grown up in a society that sees a disabling illness as an unmentionable tragedy and refers to people as 'wheelchair-bound' or 'confined to a wheelchair' instead of seeing the wheelchair as a liberating tool, it is impossible not to be affected by these attitudes.

Joanne was able to illustrate from her own experience in bringing up two children born a number of years apart how a disabled person's perception of their own situation can change. Although she was better able to walk when the first child was small, she went out and about with her only when strictly necessary – to do the shopping or to take her daughter to school

– because the effort of walking was so exhausting. By the time her second child was born her walking ability had decreased and she had bought a battery-operated scooter. 'Chris and I enjoy roaming around on the scooter. When my daughter was small I didn't volunteer to help at the school because I knew it would be too much physically. Now I help with fêtes, jumble sales, whatever's going on. At the playschool, it's me who goes off over the fields after errant children or who supervises a game of ball on the field. It would have been better if I had had the scooter when Jane was small but in those days I didn't feel that I needed it.'

Children frequently inject their own enthusiasm for gadgets, gismos and anything with wheels into a parent's feelings about the equipment they use – take the boy who asked his father when he would be old enough to have his own wheelchair, for example, or the children who love to swing on their mother's 'monkey pole' bed hoist. My own daughter as a baby transformed my first experience of using a wheelchair on a potentially difficult aeroplane trip. She sat on my lap and gave big beaming smiles to the airport staff who were pushing me. She set up the link between them and me and so the experience I had dreaded became enjoyable.

Another first was less positive, 'I'll never forget the first time I used a wheelchair so that we could go shopping in Milton Keynes. The classic thing that everyone says about people speaking to the person pushing the wheelchair and not the person in it turned out to be true. My husband pushed me up to the door of the womens' toilets and then I was getting up to use my sticks to go in. A woman, wanting to be helpful, said to him, 'Can she manage or shall I give her a hand?'

One woman, who walks mainly unaided but occasionally uses crutches or a wheelchair, said that, in her experience, 'If you are on crutches people try to be helpful. If you're in a wheelchair they ignore you'. In contrast, another's experience with using crutches had been more awkward: 'When people first see you they say cheerily, "What happened to you then?", thinking you're getting over an accident. When you tell them you've got MS they get all apologetic and the jokey atmosphere disappears. A sudden hush descends'.

'Much more of a sticking point for me than using a wheelchair is getting hand controls for the car. It's partly financial, partly the thought that it would affect my husband too and partly the finality of it. Once I'd done it that would be that.' For another person the transition from using one stick to using two, or the thought of using a catheter might be the 'sticking point'. Others who have been that route already were able to vouch for the liberation it has brought them.

'When Alistair was still small I started to use a catheter which turned out to be a great improvement in the organisation of life with a baby. It was simpler than juggling between changing a dirty nappy or struggling to get to the toilet in time myself. It's easier to go out, if you don't have to worry about where the loos are all the time.'

THE WEAKEST LINK

The access that a disabled parent has to activities within and beyond the family is determined by the weakest link, so to speak, in the chain of people, places and events that go to make up that activity. That link may be physical, for example a doorway that is too narrow to admit a wheelchair; it may be organisational, as when a child is allocated to an upstairs classroom without anyone noticing that this will prevent the parent from visiting; it may be a question of information – when an event is perfectly accessible but the disabled person has no way of knowing that it is taking place; or it may be structural, as when for example a parent does not fit the criteria to qualify for a vital piece of equipment. It may be that everything else is in place but that there is a psychological barrier to using a particular piece of equipment or accepting some form of help. Paying attention to the weakest link is the key to access.

CHAPTER EIGHT

Allies

SOURCES OF SUPPORT

'The local community is a very positive environment for bringing up children. There's an open door policy between the parents . . . Dave's parents often have the children at weekends. The fact that they can help out if necessary or if we need a break is a great help.'

Alison

'I never really found that there was a problem with nappies or clothes. If I couldn't do it I'd put them in the pram with their buttons undone and wheel them down to someone who could!'

Annie

I made a point of asking every parent, who had been most useful to them in their parenting. The responses suggested that support from family, friends and social groups focused around, for example, schools, churches or neighbourhood was felt by many to have a more central role in their lives than formal service providers. This is not a surprising finding given that disabled parents set store by joining in, keeping going and being part of the mainstream of family life.

Getting support from within the family, neighbourhood or a self-selected social grouping has a number of advantages. It is to hand; it is flexible; arrangements can be changed at the last minute when the need arises; there are no forms to fill in or assessment procedures to undergo; there are no labels attached.

The disabled person remains in control. Such support is acceptable because, rather than setting the family apart as being different or problematical, it is consistent with the way most families operate. It is part of a relationship of give and take with all that that implies in terms of exchange and mutuality.

Balanced against this is the view expressed by several people that they would prefer not to be reliant on family members, friends and neighbours for help. 'I'd rather keep them as friends and neighbours, not scare them off. I would only really use them in emergencies.' For others, community support is simply not available. 'The immediate neighbours are elderly on one side and unhelpful on the other . . . My family have not involved themselves. They brought me up to be independent and they're not around much. It's not their way.'

It would be misleading and counter-productive if findings about the significance of community support were taken as evidence that support from statutory sources is not important. Rather, the points to be drawn out are these. First, the choice about who helps and what form that help takes should remain with the disabled parent. It has already been pointed out that this is a principle within the NHS & Community Care Act but all too seldom a reality. Second, statutory support which has the characteristics of the best organic support available within the community will be much more highly valued by disabled parents than that which requires them to fit themselves to the needs and requirements of organisations.[1]

A way also has to be found to loosen the association between social services support and the stigma of implied neediness. A number of parents expressed wariness about social workers. 'I don't believe in social workers unless I really need one', and, 'I try not to have much to do with social services' were comments typical of this attitude. There was no evidence that this was because the professionals in this particular group were more inept or less sensitive than others. As with midwives, doctors, specialists, nurses, health visitors, teachers and occupational therapists, a mixture of experiences was reported; some individuals had been helpful, some had not. The caution seemed to stem from the strong association between needing a social worker and being seen to have problems.

Ultimately, it is understood that social services have the power to remove children from their parents. One mother came to an abrupt and shocking realisation of this when she was informed by her doctor that she would qualify for a social services' home care assistant. When she expressed her surprise and satisfaction that this resource was available to her, the doctor replied, that social services would far rather pay for a home care assistant than end up taking her children into care. 'He said it quite casually, but to me it was a bombshell. I'd never for one moment thought of anything like that happening.' This particular doctor had not thought about the effect his words would have, and social services certainly cannot be held responsible for his lack of tact, but the fact is that he was putting into words what many parents consider to be 'the bottom line'.

Working experience of the Children Act of 1989 and the NHS & Community Care Act of 1990 suggests that there is a potential tension between the social services role in support of parents and their role as protectors of children.[2] This was realised by at least one mother, and made her extremely wary of social services. 'It became clear to me that a family aide, whose role was to befriend and gain the mother's confidence, was also expected to report back to social services and she was giving them an interpretation of the situation that I did not agree with. After that I really didn't want to know.' The dual role of the worker, expected both to befriend and to report on the mother, made the relationship unworkable in her opinion.

Sometimes a situation arises where the social or health worker has their own agenda and defines the situation in a way that seems to the parent to allow the professional inappropriate control. 'The home-helps complained that they were being asked to do too much work in the time they had been allocated. I felt that this confirmed that not enough time had been allocated in the first place but the care manager said that I shouldn't be carrying on with my degree. When that problem was out of the way, the hours were increased, but not when I said so.' In the end, Kate had four and a half hours of assistance from social services and paid someone for a further seven to eight hours help, which she could have at the times of her choice and use in whatever way suited her without having to account to social services for her actions and choices. For most parents this would not be an option unless as part of a direct payment scheme, like those discussed in the previous chapter.

WHAT MAKES A PROFESSIONAL AN ALLY?

The four main characteristics of good professional–parent interactions to emerge from the interviews were as follows: providing encouragement; supporting a parent's way of doing things; helping to find solutions to practical challenges and; opening doors to resources. Each of these is explored below.

Providing encouragement

> *'Of my outsiders the best was Christine, my health visitor. She always gave me really good moral support, she insisted, "Shirley you* are *a mum". She was always positive and somehow, by her manner, put you at ease.'*

> Shirley

The health visitor's expressions of confidence in her mothering meant a great deal to Shirley, whilst Jan, in hospital with her first baby, drew strength from the comment of a midwife, 'That baby will only ever know you as its mother'. The effects of a timely word of encouragement upon any new parent cannot be overestimated; all the more so when that parent has been exposed to expressions of doubt about their ability to cope and has had few opportunities, like Paula quoted below, to compare notes with other parents.

'The health visitor came quite a lot in the early days. She didn't offer much in the way of practical help but she kept morale up, telling me that I was just as good a parent, if not better, than other mothers. It was really important to me that she said that. Life at that stage was not pleasurable, just sheer hard work.'

The social isolation of some disabled parents means that the role of the professional in providing encouragement and information can be particularly important. At the same time it is important to recognise that it can never be a substitute for peer contact. The best encouragement a professional can supply may be to do as my own doctor did and give one disabled parent the opportunity to make contact with another (see Chapter One).

Equal to the power of the positive word is the damaging potential of a negative one. 'A teacher took Ben on one side and said, "It can't be very easy for you having disabled parents". He came out with it in an argument one day. I've done my damnedest to give them a normal childhood. I felt all my efforts had been undermined by that one teacher.'

Supporting a parent's way of doing things

'I break every rule in the book. I started spoon feeding my first baby at six weeks. My health visitor expressed disapproval but she shut up when I told her that I was spoon-fed from birth because I was born with no roof to my mouth. I said to her, "Have babies changed since then?" I've only had phone contact with the new one so far but it sounds quite promising. It sounds as though she'll support me in what I decide to do . . . '

Annie

Professionals are often working with a disabled mother for the first time and have no repertoire of relevant experience to draw on. This does not necessarily limit their value to the parent, provided that a good relationship is established and the expertise of the mother is properly valued. How that relationship operates might vary greatly from one individual to another. Liz described two very different health visitors. The first 'was always coming round to check up on me'. Her interventions were seen as well meaning but intrusive. This was contrasted with the approach of a second health visitor who came round much less often and who Liz felt comfortable with because, 'she was willing to let me get on'. By contrast, Karen liked the way that her health visitor 'was always dropping in and would bring all her students to meet me'.

Some parents choose to keep contact with external agencies and officialdom to a minimum whilst others take the greatest possible advantage of the resources and facilities on offer because they feel that this is the best way to optimise the quality of life for themselves and their children. From the first point of view, a good professional would be one who keeps her or his distance whilst remaining approachable. From the second point of view a good professional would be one that makes a point of keeping in touch, providing useful information and efficiently linking the family with appropriate resources. Although there are parents at both extremes of welcoming and avoiding contact with professionals, most parents steer a course somewhere in between.

One mother might be delighted to have someone else look after her children for a while so that she can rest or get on with something else. To another, the idea of an outsider's help with the children is unacceptable because she feels that it would undermine her own role in the family. Annie found it useful that her older boy was given a place at a social services' day nursery when she was expecting her second child but she preferred not to have outside helpers in the home. 'I was jealous of the way I did things. I hated the idea of anyone coming in and taking over. I would rather do without the help than have it in a form that made me feel undermined.'

Professionals work within their own constraints; the requirement upon a health visitor to carry out certain developmental tests for example, or the tension within the social worker's role between supporting parents and overseeing the welfare of children. The danger is that a parent's reluctance to enter into a working relationship with any given agency may be interpreted as a problem with their parenting when in fact the real issue is the relationship between the parent and the service provider.

Things work best where there is flexibility about the level of professional involvement so that this can be determined at a level which is neither massively more nor lamentably less than the parent feels comfortable with. Clearly there is no 'right' or 'wrong' approach, but rather a need for a responsive interaction with individual families. But whilst there can be no single approach, there does have to be a consistent underlying principle; namely to affirm the disabled parent in their role. Kate's experience is there to be learnt from: 'When helpers arrived, I would hand over the baby to them and say, "Get on with it – I need a break!" When the helper had gone I'd have to start all over again from scratch with the baby. It meant I never really built up confidence in myself as a mother.'

Helping to find solutions to practical challenges

'Each new difficulty that came up, we had to work the answer out for ourselves.'

Jan

'It feels strange, having a toddler to look after once again, but we'll learn as we go along, like we did with Hannah. You work around things. If you think a child is going to be stroppy at the shops then you don't take them! You have to plan ahead and take more precautions . . . '

Mary

When health or social welfare professionals say to new disabled mothers or fathers, 'However will you cope?', their minds may be racing swiftly over a variety of scenarios: changing a baby's nappy, going after a runaway toddler, getting a sleeping child into bed and so on. The parents will probably have faced all these challenges in their own imaginations, plus a great many more.

It is often harder for the onlooker to imagine how these

practicalities might be dealt with than it is for the disabled person, who in many cases has years of experience of living and working in an environment that is not well suited to their physical needs. Many of the interviewees who had been disabled for some time had considerable expertise in assessing equipment and getting hold of it, making adaptations, and working out solutions to the particular challenges which they faced.

Very few of the parents I spoke to, however, had had the opportunity to share ideas with others in a similar situation (a number commented that I was the only other disabled parent they had come across). For the most part they had had to start from scratch in finding solutions to the practical difficulties they faced. Professionals who had been able and willing to help with this process were valued: 'The midwives were helpful in finding ways round practical problems and helping with adaptations'. However, another mother's experience had been less positive: 'After the birth it was a real struggle to establish a position for breastfeeding. All sorts of impractical and painful suggestions were made and duly carried out. Eventually, after I came home I discovered a perfectly easy solution, resting the baby on a pillow which could be readily moved from one side to the other'.

Some mothers described not so much a lack of willingness to help, as a failure of imagination. Kate, who has cerebral palsy, had been taken into hospital a week early because the midwives thought she should get some help in preparing to look after the baby. 'They gave me a doll to practise on. As preparation it was useless because dolls don't move – the problem was – babies do!'

Professionals in the maternity services cannot be expected to know everything about a huge range of impairments and conditions, but parents are naturally sensitive towards the degree of thought that has been given to their situation. 'The midwives kept insisting that I would be better off if I got up and walked around. I had to explain to them that I just couldn't do that because it would leave me in pain. Once I explained, they accepted it.' Marion's medical notes stated that she had a condition that affected her ankles but it was not until the actual birth that any attention was given to the practical implications of this.

The government sponsored report, *Changing Childbirth*,[3] emphasises the importance of continuity of care in the maternity services. This is an important principle for all women but the evidence from these interviews suggests that it is especially important in the case of disabled mothers in order that they do not find themselves in the position of having to divide their attention between giving birth, looking after a newborn baby and advising professionals about the details of their own physical needs.

Doctors who are specialists in a particular condition or impairment frequently know little or nothing about pregnancy and childbirth, and few childbirth experts have experience of disability, so that it is difficult for parents to come by specific information relating impairment and maternity. This is one area where peer contact and information exchange between disabled parents and health professionals (see Chapter Ten) are making a crucial difference to the support available.

Opening doors to resources

'I would have liked more information at the outset. To have been told exactly what help was available. Once you know what's there you can ask for it but nobody tells you, they wait for you to ask. They see you coping and leave it at that.'

Paula

'My GP admits that he himself cannot help, but he's always prepared to make referrals and in that sense he's very helpful.'

Helen

I asked each parent which professionals they had found most useful to them in their parenting and was struck by the wide range of answers given. There were no clear winners in terms of any type of professional being seen as more useful or generally speaking more enlightened than any other. What was clear however was that it was important to parents that there should be one or more professionals in whom they felt they could place their confidence. For example, for Marion finding a consultant that she trusted proved a real breakthrough. 'I have an excellent consultant. It was a bumpy road to get to him but now I've got someone I feel confident with I would never change.' Having one good ally puts other, less useful, relationships in perspective. Marion went on, 'I don't waste time going to the doctor because there's nothing he can do in any case . . . The health visitors where I lived before were really helpful but here I don't see anything of them. I can't take Rachel to the clinic, so she doesn't get weighed, but that doesn't bother me'.

Annette, who was wary of contact with social workers, was nonetheless happy to make extensive use of 'my OT' [occupational therapist] and commented on how readily the doctor made time for her if she ever needed to see him. Mary and Sam indicated that, for them, social services would be the first place they would go to if any practical issues needed resolving. 'We've always found them helpful, though within certain limits and constraints.' The fact that Sam has worked in a social services department and 'knows his way round the system', probably leads to greater confidence in their dealings with social workers than was generally the case.

Part of the role of the 'key' professional can be to point the way towards other useful people and/or resources: 'If I want to get hold of anything or anyone I generally find that a letter from the doctor will do it', or again, 'When Alistair was having problems with a bossy teacher the health visitor drew in the GP. He intervened and got the matter sorted'.

What the job title of the worker is does not seem to matter; it could be the doctor for one person, the health visitor for another, an occupational therapist, social worker or district nurse for others, but for most people it does seem to be important to have someone there who feels as though they are on the parent's side and who can act as a 'first port of call'.

The selection by the parent of a professional who can play a central supporting role is a natural process based partly on compatibility of approach and partly on convenience. This is fine when it occurs naturally but it does not always happen automatically. The degree of support received may depend on an individual discovering what is available and working out how to access it.

It is interesting to consider whether the notion of a 'key' professional supporting a disabled parent could or should be formalised. A starting point might be to look at those relationships where contact takes place as a matter of course: health visitors for parents of under fives and GPs for virtually everyone, though a mother who does not need to visit the doctor and no longer has contact with the health visitor, because her child or children are over five, may not have access to this kind of information and support unless the professional makes a point of keeping in touch. Beth mentioned that her doctor would regularly 'pop in to see how things were going'. Shirley and Karen both described how their health visitors, having built up a good relationship, had stayed in touch even after their formal role had ended, one having retired and the other having moved to a different area.

These professionals have a role as potential 'brokers' in that they are in a position to alert a new parent or a newly-disabled parent to the range of resources and to point them in the direction of people who can make those resources available. Ideally this would leave the parent themselves in a position to specify who they want to use as their main point of access and ongoing support.

The Greatest Challenge: summary of the group portrait

'I find that the greatest challenge is balancing my independence with my dependence.'

Sally

Sally put her finger on a question which in one form or another ran through the interviews – how do you achieve a balance between dependence and independence? How do you retain a sense of being in control whilst using help from other people? Whatever the strategy of the individual parent or family, what mattered was being able to maintain a sense of control and to do this as far as possible within a context of give as well as take.

The balance had to be struck on a number of levels: within oneself, in partnerships, in relation to families and friends and in relation to external agencies of support. There were as many different approaches as there were interviewees. Whilst some gained a sense of control by managing their family life with as little help as possible, others found it in the challenge of coordinating a veritable team of helpers. Many described a situation in which they had come to terms with the level of practical support they needed without losing their self-respect. A few were struggling with the feeling that they were losing control of their lives. Often where there was a diminished sense of control this was linked to a diminished sense of self-worth, brought about by the loss, for example, of a much-valued job, or through the lack of opportunities to be with other adults.

Despite differences of situation and approach, there was a marked and widespread agreement about goals. A keynote throughout the interviews was the drive towards achieving the fullest and most satisfying lifestyle possible. Within this common goal, attitudes and tactical priorities varied considerably. Annette and Helen provided examples of contrasting strategies.

Annette and family steadfastly rejected the label of 'disability' and accepted as little help from outside the immediate family as possible, even if this meant foregoing resources they might otherwise have had access to. Though there might be a price to pay in terms of the sheer physical struggle of day-to-day living, the successful completion of physical tasks, unremarkable for others, was a source of enormous satisfaction to Annette. Helen and family made every possible accommodation to lessen the disabling consequences of illness. The labels and procedures, however time-consuming or vexing at times, were taken on so that the family could capitalise as fully as possible on resources and support. But the two women described their aims in virtually identical words – to enable the family to live 'as normal a life as possible'.

There are two dimensions to the pursuit of 'normality'; first, that disabled parents do not want attention drawn to their lives as though they were different from everybody else's, that is they do not want to be *outlined*, but second, that they do not want to be *sidelined* because social, physical or attitudinal barriers prevent their full participation. They wish to assert their right not only to have children but also to join in as fully as they choose in family and community life.

In a society that regards self-sufficiency as a social virtue, parents who manage without help tend to be regarded as the most competent, while those who draw upon support outside the immediate family are regarded as managing less well and may even be construed as being 'at risk'. But is the most effective parent the one that asks for the least help and involves the fewest people in their family life, or is an effective parent one who is successful in drawing in appropriate support and resources to augment and enrich those of the immediate family? Many of those I spoke with had become very skillful at drawing other adults and young people into their family life. Disabled parents are less likely to go along with the view that self-reliance is the ultimate parental virtue and more likely to recognise the value to children and adults alike of living in families where close, familial type relationships are developed with people beyond the immediate biological family unit. This is humorously illustrated by the title of Micheline Mason's essay on her experiences as a single, disabled parent, 'A nineteen-parent family'.[4]

113

This is not a book about heroines and heroes; but neither does it set out to demonstrate how 'normal' disabled parents and their families are. That would be to overlook the extent to which our situation challenges society's expectations of disabled people and the effort and energy we continually expend in overcoming barriers that get in the way as we go about our family lives. It would also overlook the features of our parenting which we consider distinctive and worth learning from.

So what is the reality? Are our families characterised by their normality, their abnormality or their exceptionality? Are disabled parents concerned with fighting a rear-guard action, merging into the mainstream or signalling a way forward which other parents would do well to follow? What deserves to be celebrated is neither our 'normality' nor our 'difference' but our distinctive contribution to ending the oppressive conditions experienced by all parents.

The idea of normality is most useful when it can be balanced against an appreciation of what is distinctive about the experience of families in which one or both parents are disabled. One thing that is clear is that it does not make sense to go after a supposed normality that will involve the disabled parent in continuous uncomplaining struggle. Drawing attention to the barriers and prejudices faced by this particular group of parents and prospective parents society may be moved in a direction that will benefit all parents of young children.

Building Networks
of Support

CHAPTER NINE

Meeting

BARRIERS TO MEETING

*'It's impossible to plan when you don't know from
one day to the next how much energy you'll have.'*
Helen

I asked each of the parents I spoke with if they would be interested in meeting as a group to discuss some of the issues raised. On the whole there was a very positive response to the idea and so a meeting was finally arranged about six months after the last of the interviews, with the local social services department agreeing to meet the costs, including transport to and from the meeting. In the event just nine people came. The reasons for non-attendance illustrate many of the reasons, both practical and psychological, why it is often difficult for disabled parents to get together.

The range of venues which have both good disabled access and facilities for small children is limited and the hunt for a suitable and affordable place to meet can be a barrier at the very outset. Sometimes venues that would work from a practical point of view, such as a social services day centre or a rehabilitation unit, have to be ruled out because their medical and social welfare associations make them unacceptable venues for a parents' group.

A number of parents had fluctuating or limited energy levels. A meeting that involves several hours away from home was out of the question for some. Several people expressed reluctance to risk overtiring themselves, especially where long journeys and transfers in and out of taxis were involved. Joanne said that she preferred to conserve her limited energies for looking after her family.

Transport is a major constraint in terms of organisation and cost as well as energy expenditure. The group included several people living in rural areas and so the transport costs were high and potentially, if more people had attended, very high indeed. Without social services or other funding the meeting would have been out of the question. Family economics are affected by disability and this can be a further barrier to contact. Take Julie, for example, who had, with mixed feelings, taken a part-time job in order to be able to pay the extra rent on an accessible council bungalow the family had recently moved into.

Apart from energy constraints there were health issues for a number of parents, illustrating how both unforeseen events and the uncertainty of health service schedules make planning difficult. Helen was in hospital, following a recent fall and Annette could not arrange to go out for the day because she was waiting for a hospital appointment to become available. Annie had also been in hospital, but for an entirely positive reason. She sent word that she had given birth to a daughter the previous week.

Paula said that she preferred not to be involved because, as she put it, 'I finally have the sense that the worst of my struggles are over and I can get on with my life'. Many disabled parents take pride in having succeeded as parents in spite of the initial doubts and fears of family, friends and professionals. For some this means that they think twice about drawing attention to their situation and risking giving out the impression that they have problems.

Chris felt that whilst she welcomed the idea of meeting with other disabled parents for herself, she would not want to involve her children. 'They accept my disability but I don't know how they'd react if they saw me with other disabled people.' Like a number of others I spoke to, Chris had never belonged to any group with disability as its focus.

The fact that it was a meeting for parents made it feel comfortable to some, in spite of the link with disability, though Karen said, 'I wonder whether it's a good idea to isolate yourself into a group of disabled people. I feel more like an able-bodied person in any case'.

Many disabled parents prefer not to think of themselves as belonging to an identifiable sub-section of parents. It is difficult for anyone who does not think of themselves as being disabled to feel comfortable about joining a group which has disability as part of its focus. The less opportunity an individual has had to be with other disabled people, the stronger the anxiety, very often, not to be seen as disabled. Meeting with others threatens to bring one face-to-face with an unacceptable identity. Even some of those who say that they have no difficulty thinking of themselves as disabled, still prefer not to involve themselves with other disabled people, fearing that they will become associated in other people's minds with a particular social minority and cease to be seen as regular parents.

Kate stayed at home in order to meet the deadline on a book she was writing. She was in any case not sure that she would have wanted to come. A few years earlier she and her husband attended a weekend organised by a charity to bring together four sets of parents with cerebral palsy. She had found it a demoralising experience: 'The whole thing was a failure. It was a random group of people with different educational backgrounds, children of different ages. All the others had girls and none of them seemed to have any problems. I came away feeling totally depressed. It's a misconception that people with disabilities will automatically have things in common. Having children is a fact of life, not a common interest'.

MEETINGS OF THE INTERVIEWEES

'It's been good, having the chance to hear other people's stories.'

Chris

119

At the first meeting three people had agreed to lead discussions on different subjects: talking to the children about illness and disability; the issues for partners (this discussion was led by a non-disabled partner) and issues around access.

Towards the end of the meeting each person was asked to say briefly if they would like the group to continue and if so, on what lines. The feeling of the group was that there would be interest in meeting again at some point, though it was felt that it was neither necessary nor a good use of energies to meet too frequently. Several people said that they had found it fascinating to listen to one anothers' stories, both where these rang bells and where they touched on unfamiliar themes. Getting together provided evidence of not being 'the only one' and helped to counter the isolation felt by many.

Some people felt that they would like to keep in touch between meetings with other parents who were in similar circumstances or dealing with common issues such as getting wheelchair access in their childrens' schools.

The group met again the following year. Numbers were roughly constant, though there were several changes in who was there. In the meantime I had been in touch with most of the group. My reasons for making contact included piloting a postal questionnaire for the Maternity Alliance and checking draft portions of this book. Though no formal local contact network had developed, several people had joined the national contact register of disabled parents which is held by ParentAbility (see Chapter Ten).

A few months later several families living in the same area got together with their families for lunch and extended the invitation to other disabled parents they knew of. A year further on a third meeting was held. This time attendance was down to a handful but a specific focus emerged, since three of the five mothers who came expressed an interest in doing disability awareness-raising work in schools in the area. It was decided to do this in conjunction with the local organisation of disabled people which was in the process of setting up a training team.

120

This suited the needs and interests of this group of individuals, whose children were all of school age, but there was still no group for new parents. Two years later a social worker based at a day centre spotted the absence of any kind of organised facility for disabled parents and, in conjunction with a local mother, set up a monthly drop-in group which attracted several parents of babies and pre-schoolers. These parents are, at the time of writing, seeking funding to run as an independent group.

TWO SUPPORT GROUPS FOR DISABLED PARENTS

It is interesting to compare what has happened in my own area with the story of two other support groups set up by disabled mothers elsewhere in the country. Although each group began in a different way and evolved its own objectives, there are comparisons to be made, particularly in relation to the difficulty of making and sustaining contact, the way in which groups develop and the value of the groups both to their own members and others.

PANDA in Norfolk

> *'I know what it's like to feel that you're the only one. I didn't want anyone else to have to go through what I'd been through.'*
>
> Kathy Saunders, founder of PANDA

Dealing with a young child and a new baby, on top of having just moved into an area where she had no established network of support, proved so traumatic for Kathy Saunders that she resolved to set up a support group for others in a similar situation. 'I felt I had to start by finding another mum who might have experienced similar difficulties. This was a big problem because I didn't know any other disabled parents at all. One day by pure chance I saw someone in the street. The first time I couldn't bring myself to talk to this stranger; it seemed such a dreadful invasion – a

121

crude accusation of similarity based purely on physical characteristics – I still cringe when I think about it. When this same woman passed me again about ten minutes later I thought, "Now or never", and stopped her. I blurted out that I needed help to start a group for parents with disabilities, gave her my telephone number and asked her to contact me if she felt any interest in the idea. I didn't really expect to hear from her but she did phone . . . '

The two women went about developing contacts with local voluntary and statutory services and before long had succeeded in building up a 'starter' group of disabled parents with a committee and a simple constitution. They made the decision to include partners and other family members in the group. They set out to have as high a profile as they could and took every opportunity to spread word of their existence, including printing and distributing 3000 leaflets.

The nature of PANDA has evolved in response to what works best for those involved. The organising group noticed that monthly meetings were not well attended. Rather than further isolate those who could not get out to the meetings they stuck to quarterly open business meetings with an AGM and an autumn party. A quarterly newsletter is sent out which, 'although it is a lot of work, keeps us together'.

A key feature of the group's work, 'which necessarily centres on a few key individuals,' is passing on and exchanging information, whether directly to disabled parents, to health and social welfare workers in the area or within the national network of disabled parents. PANDA's experience as the oldest continuing local self-help group for disabled parents means that their advice is widely sought by others who are attempting to set up groups of their own.

The group has undertaken a survey of disabled parents, mostly drawing on the experience of parents living in East Anglia, which was published in the form of a report called 'Families First'.[1]

Kingston

'You could see the look of relief on a person's face when they walked into the group for the first time and realised they were not alone.'

Alison Craske, founder of Kingston group

Alison, a disabled mother living in Kingston, found herself fighting the local council to be allowed to take her young daughter with her on a 'shopmobility' scooter. In point of fact she lost the battle over access but through the resulting publicity she made contact with a number of other disabled mothers living in the area. Their children were all small and they started to meet together on a regular basis.

Alison says that a fundamental reason for setting up the group was to counter the isolation many disabled mothers experience. This group of mothers, who had become friends, asked other disabled mothers who they met to join them. They also advertised the existence of the group through the local council of disabled people. At its peak the group numbered about ten and was meeting about every two weeks.

A limitation of a group organised on the basis of affinity, Alison feels, is that it is difficult to accommodate people whose situation or outlook is very different from that of the existing members. A woman came to the group for a few sessions who made other members feel uncomfortable, 'she wanted to help everybody all the time; it was as though she saw us as being more needy than her. People were relieved when she stopped coming'.

As their children began to start school, the group began to meet less often and numbers gradually tailed off, with mothers leaving the area, going back to part-time work or having other tasks and interests occupying more of their time. For some, health factors also played a part in curtailing their involvement.

Alison regards it as 'both a strength and a drawback of such a group that its priorities will inevitably change over time'. She has felt concerned that whilst new mothers still appear on the scene from time to time, there are not enough women with

123

small children to keep a regular mother and toddler type group going. 'I feel sorry that there is no longer a group for them to be part of.'

THE FORMATION OF LOCAL GROUPS[2]

> *'Self-help groups were slow to develop . . . but they have flourished and become a powerful source of mutual support, education and action among people affected by particular health concerns or disabilities . . . while learning and working together, disabled people can combine their power to influence social and political decisions that affect their lives.'*[3]

Around the country, other groups and local networks of disabled parents have been forming at more or less the same time as those described above. At the time of writing there are probably between twenty and thirty such groups, most of which have formed within the last ten years.

Typically, groups form when one disabled parent looks for others in a similar situation. Often, the first move has been taken by a health visitor, social worker or other professional. In the north of the country a mixed group is seeking to establish a network of disabled parents and interested professionals.

Some groups have a specific focus (for example, deaf parents or mothers with visual impairments) whilst others are general. Some are small groups of people who know each other well, meet regularly and consider each other as friends. Other groups are more diffuse and geographically widespread. In such cases social functions often take second place to information sharing and giving support in specific situations. Telephone contact and letter writing play more of a role than face-to-face meetings. The aims and scope of groups vary according to where they are located, the stage of parenting those involved are at and how much support is available to the group.

The need for certain types of contact remains constant – for example, there will always be new disabled mothers who would find it useful to meet with others – but the needs of a particular group of individuals inevitably changes as children grow older and family life enters new phases. A group that originally met as a mother and toddler group will eventually find that members are discussing the challenges of parenting teenagers!

Fluctuations in health and other changes in the situation of group members call for flexibility in the way things are organised. Groups have shown imagination in finding ways of staying in touch; using telephone contact, letter exchange, newsletters and experimenting with the timing and organisation of meetings such as getting together in smaller units with only occasional meetings of the larger group.

There is a difference between a group which exists for the benefit of its immediate members and one which offers itself as a wider resource, although it can happen that a group that starts out as the former ends up as the latter and this has significant implications in terms of the resources the group will need.

Some groups, like PANDA, have deliberately gone for having a high profile locally. This makes sense where a major focus of the group is awareness raising or when the group is running campaigns on specific issues such as wheelchair access to local schools, equality awareness training for school staff and so on.

Once their existence becomes known, groups may find that they are faced with numerous and often urgent demands for information, support and, in some cases, counselling. It is clearly important that groups like this, which are providing a public service that is not otherwise available, receive adequate financial backing and have access to such training as they feel they need. Frequently good links are made with health and social welfare professionals and with those involved in parent and child support. There is a shortage of information in this area and professionals are often grateful to find a source of accurate and up-to-date information.

The move towards encouraging user control of resources has had an effect on the policy of many social service departments so that increasingly the decision is taken to support existing and new self-help groups in place of setting up initiatives run by service providers. Both parents and professionals recognise the value of external support that facilitates rather than replaces the leadership of disabled parents themselves.

As well as collecting relevant local information, some groups act as a source of information about national resources, such as ParentAbility's contact register and resource list. Some groups have established contact with other disabled parent groups; sharing experiences and exchanging ideas.

THE STRENGTHS OF A COLLECTIVE APPROACH

'We have to shout!'

Shirley Ellis, disabled mother

Whatever the difficulties in coming together and the constraints upon what is done, the potential benefits are great. First and foremost, being together counters the sense of isolation which many disabled parents experience. Second, the numbers involved provide a sound and incontrovertible basis for challenging the belief (or tacit assumption rather) that disabled parents do not exist in any numbers and that no provision need therefore be made for their needs. Third, it is possible to pool information about experiences; resources that have been found useful or not useful and equipment that has been discovered, adapted or rejected. This multi-dimensional information base can be useful both in support of one another and in relation to those who see it as their job to provide support. It gives a platform from which to challenge inadequate provision and promote good practice, and establish the status of disabled parents, which was always there but not always recognised, as experts in their own situation.[4]

This, and the following two chapters describe a piece of history in the making – how disabled parents are finding personal confidence and collective strength; working together with individual and organisational allies to improve the antenatal provision, maternity services and parent support available to disabled people.

CHAPTER TEN

Developing a Self-help Network

PARENTABILITY

> *'If they could be put in touch with someone who's been through a similar situation . . . even if you don't want to be friends with them, just to be able to pick their brains about what you need, find useful, how you can get yourself organised to do the things you want to do.'*

> *'There is no information, apart from the standard information you get from books you're given when you first become pregnant . . . Health Education books which deal entirely from the viewpoint of able-bodied people.'*

> Disabled mothers[1]

In 1982 a disabled couple sought the support of the National Childbirth Trust (NCT) to set up a self-help group for disabled parents. Jenny Estermann wrote of the negativity she had encountered from family, health and social welfare personnel as she became first a mother and later a foster parent. The couple contacted the NCT after hearing that its 'Postnatal Committee' had begun looking into the situation of disabled parents within the NCT as part of its response to the International Year of the Disabled in 1981.

A newsletter was sent out jointly by the Estermanns and the Postnatal Committee to all the disabled parents they were in contact with at that point. The Postnatal Committee produced a booklet, *The Emotions and Experiences of Some Mothers with Disabilities*[2] based on interviews with twenty disabled mothers. Before its publication they held a study day to look in more detail at some of the issues raised by the research. Personal experiences recounted by the disabled parents present were a central feature of the day. A working group, which included disabled mothers, was formed to take forward some of the recommendations that had come out of the research and study day.

There were other indications that the subject of disabled parents was beginning to receive attention. Between 1984 and 1986 three other organisations held study days with a direct bearing on the subject of disabled parents.[3,4,5] Reports from these events suggested that there were two different ways of talking about the lives of disabled parents. Whilst service providers used the language of 'needs assessment' and 'problems', disabled parents favoured the language of participation and stressed that they saw themselves as part of the mainstream, 'as normal parents getting on with our lives'. In order for this to be possible they wanted enough, and the right kind of, resources and support: affordable, flexible and provided in a non-patronising manner. 'I just want to have ordinary life experiences with people and not have to use them and, as long as I am practically and physically supported, it is perfectly possible to lead some semblance of a normal life as well as looking after my baby.'[6]

What emerged from the interviews and study days was that many parents felt isolated, with little access either to other disabled parents or to relevant information. The working group decided that their first priority should be to set up a national 'contact register' through which disabled parents could get in touch with others in similar situations, some of whom might live close enough to meet in person. Another volunteer started to compile a data-base of information about equipment, adaptations and solutions to some of the practical challenges facing disabled parents.

The women running the register and helpline noticed that they were often approached in the first instance by professionals working alongside disabled parents rather than by the parents themselves. The professionals also expressed a sense of working in isolation. It seemed appropriate to set up a professional contact register parallel to the one operating for parents so that professionals working in a variety of different contexts – medical, social welfare, educational or voluntary – could find out about others whose work in support of disabled parents related in some way to their own. Over the years an increasing number of requests came in for ParentAbility (the name chosen by the working group in 1990) to help with study days, contribute to basic professional training, provide information to students and so on.

Over a period of seven years, ParentAbility carried out three access surveys[7,8,9] and produced, with periodic up-dates, a comprehensive resource list for disabled parents.[10]

The ParentAbility contact register has grown slowly but steadily over the first decade or so of its existence and at the time of writing has about 600 members, living in England, Scotland, Wales and Northern Ireland. Over that time the composition of ParentAbility's organising group has shifted so that the majority are now disabled parents.

At the same time a number of local self-help groups for disabled parents (such as those mentioned in the previous chapter) have formed which are loosely linked to ParentAbility. It has become part of the group's style of meeting to move around the country visiting different local groups, inviting them to attend and put their own concerns on the agenda.

ParentAbility liaises extensively with other organisations, both voluntary and statutory, the media and researchers, seeking to raise awareness about the situation of disabled parents and to feed in relevant information. It has been the group's constant practice to inject expertise into relevant mainstream initiatives wherever possible.

One way in which ParentAbility has brought the issues faced

by disabled parents to a wider audience is by putting together an exhibition of visual images and words and a loan collection of drawings and photographs for use in leaflets, articles and books. The exhibition is accompanied by workshop materials which have often led into thought-provoking discussions about the role visual imagery plays in *creating* and also in *challenging* stereotypes.

Over the past eight years ParentAbility members have taken a leading role in establishing and sustaining the work of the *Maternity Alliance Disability Working Group, Disability, Pregnancy and Parenthood International (DPPI)* which is a quarterly journal; *Equipped* (an initiative aimed at improving the range of equipment and adaptations available) and *Parents Too!* (see below).

ParentAbility has had an effect far beyond what its very limited budget and unpaid membership would suggest were likely. In part this is because it has been possible to harness the energies of a strong network of volunteers around the country. The NCT's support has been crucial in enabling ParentAbility to establish an effective peer support and educational base. There is agreement between the NCT and the core team that the time is now right for ParentAbility to seek independent charitable status.

One of the advantages of this is that it would enable ParentAbility to choose where to put its energies and what role to play; where to lead an initiative; where to take a collaborative role and where to make an input into initiatives taken by other groups. It would also provide the opportunity to find ways of working and organising which are appropriate to the situation of disabled parent volunteers, working from home (see Chapter Eleven). There are no 'off the peg' solutions – the challenge is to forge a new model of volunteer support and development.

Maternity Alliance Disability Working Group

*'I had never met another disabled parent until this
weekend. It's nice to finally realise I am right to feel
the way I do. I thought I was the only one.'*
       Comment of disabled mother after attending the
             Maternity Alliance conference, *Disabled People,
                  Pregnancy and Early Parenthood*[11]

*A key principle throughout this charter is the
recognition of the central role that disabled parents
and prospective parents have in bringing about
change.'*[12]

In 1988 the Maternity Alliance Educational and Research
Trust, an umbrella group with members from a wide range of
organisations, set up a disability working group. The Maternity
Alliance Disability Working Group (MADWG) has representation from a number of statutory and voluntary bodies
concerned with disability as well as representation from trade
unions. About one third of the members are themselves
disabled, and many of these are also parents. Several members
of the group are also on the core team of ParentAbility so that
from the outset there has been a high degree of liaison and
cooperation between the two groups.

The working group is effective in raising the profile of
disabled parents' issues with policy makers and for feeding a
disability perspective into all Maternity Alliance initiatives. The
group provided the theme for the organisation's 10th
anniversary AGM. It was involved in briefing the Expert
Maternity Group at the Department of Health in the
preparation of its report *Changing Childbirth*.[13] In 1992 the
group conducted a national postal survey of disabled parents.[14]
In November of that year they held the first ever national
meeting of disabled parents.[15] Using the input from the survey
and the conference they produced a 'charter' outlining a code of
good practice.[16]

In January 1993, Mukti Jain Campion, television producer

and author of *The Baby Challenge: a handbook on pregnancy for women with a physical disability,*[17] started a new journal, *Disability, Pregnancy and Parenthood International.* The aim of this publication is to provide a bridge between disabled parents and professionals working with them, and to spread word of good practice from one country to another. The Maternity Alliance's Disability Working Group became in effect an editorial base for this unique resource.

In 1996 the group raised funding to research and develop the support available to people with learning difficulties in the maternity services. This area of parent support had attracted attention as it became clear that the general picture was of few resources and a great deal of prejudice.[18,19] The lack, with one or two notable exceptions, of examples of good practice in this area prompted the Maternity Alliance to appoint a consultant to gather information which will provide a basis for advising 'Right From the Start', as it is known.

'PARENTS TOO!'

> *'I was visited regularly by health visitors and social workers, who tried in every way possible to make me give up my baby when it arrived. The hardest part was an hour before my husband came to take me home with the baby. The social worker came with two sets of prospective foster parents. I got hold of the baby and pulled the emergency bell. My gynaecologist was nearby fortunately and took over. The social worker was ordered out of the hospital but still continued to pester me at home for another three weeks.'*
>
> Mother with cerebral palsy[20]

Paid and voluntary workers from several organisations, including ParentAbility, RADAR, the Maternity Alliance, the Family Rights Group and Values into Action are aware of the need, often in situations of great urgency, to provide information support and, in some cases, access to advocacy for disabled parents and parents with learning difficulties who find themselves at risk of losing custody of their children.

Disabled parents involved in peer support find themselves from time-to-time talking over the phone with parents facing the threat of having children removed from home by social service departments, court battles over custody or breakdowns in arrangements with statutory service providers. Whilst they offer as much support as they can, volunteers sometimes feel that it is beyond their resources to respond adequately to these complicated and often distressing emergencies.

The campaign, 'Parents Too!', was launched in 1995 in an attempt to provide a more coordinated and better resourced response in these situations. The group's priority is to produce a set of guidelines for parents explaining their rights under the Children Act 1989 and the Community Care Act 1990 and directing them towards sources of support to  tackle discrimination. Alongside this simply presented guide there is also the intention to produce a comprehensive directory of the advocacy, information and support available locally and nationally.

CHAPTER ELEVEN

Power through Participation

'Being involved has helped me to get away from the negativity around being disabled. Some of my existing skills, that I thought had been lost for ever, are now being used to benefit others and that helps to counter my feelings of isolation.'

Ruth Carter, spokesperson for ParentAbility 1996

'What do I get out of my involvement? A whole load of satisfaction. I made the decision not to go back to work so that I could spend more time with the children but in the end I haven't lost out because I've had the chance to develop new skills and I've gained experience that will count for something when I do go back into paid work . . . Sometimes as a parent it's just nice to know that the brain still works! It's done my personal confidence a lot of good. I feel I'm a different person from the one I was three years ago. It's frustrating too at times – you talk to manu-facturers and say there's a real need for this piece of equipment and they say, "yes, yes dear . . ." As far as they're concerned you don't have the clout. The other thing I've appreciated is being in a proactive group with other disabled people. Increasingly I have the sense of being part of a movement.'

Lisa Nicholls, ParentAbility's practical
helpline coordinator 1996

'I think I can honestly say that being involved with ParentAbility has changed my life. If I hadn't got involved I don't think I'd be a mature student at university now. I wouldn't have had the belief in myself. I always had opinions but mainly I would just sound off with friends in the bar. Being involved in ParentAbility has given me the confidence to stand up in front of a hundred people and say what I know, confident that they are going to listen.'

Cathy Rafferty, ParentAbility's
newsletter editor 1996

Disabled parents, spearheaded by disabled mothers, are choosing to become visible, not because it is finally completely safe to do so and prejudice and discrimination are a thing of the past, but rather because they recognise the power of being visible as a group. By creating an effective information and peer support network, disabled parents have had a direct effect on the amount and the quality of support available to disabled parents and prospective parents. Their efforts have contributed to improvements in professional practice, awareness within the voluntary sector and the beginnings of an increase in public understanding, though Lisa Nicholl's comments remind us that no-one should underestimate the amount of work still to be done.

In the process there have been significant gains for those who have chosen to get involved. The most obvious of these is the breaking down of isolation through contact with other disabled parents. Confidence increases and skills develop as individuals take on tasks such as passing on information to another parent, making a presentation at a study day, writing an article or liaising with another organisation on a specific project. Participation can open the door to other opportunities for education, training, paid or voluntary work.

The personal development of volunteers is always significant whatever the context because it enhances the individual's sense of self-worth and frequently leads to an increase in opportunities, but all the more so when the individuals concerned have, as mothers and as disabled people, been excluded from opportunities for training and employment and as a consequence feel undervalued and disempowered (see Chapter Five).

Having effectively put the subject of disabled parents on the agenda, the central issue now facing disabled parent activists and their allies, is how to provide appropriate support and adequate resources for disabled parent volunteers working from home. Each element of this description – *disabled*, *parent*, *volunteer* and *working from home* has implications in terms of the support needed and these are explored below.

DISABLED PEOPLE AS VOLUNTEERS

It can be a positive advantage to a group which includes one or more disabled volunteers that it becomes necessary to think carefully about the most practical and effective way of going about the work. 'Because we've always done it that way' is no longer a good enough reason.

Energy constraints and the complications caused by inaccessible transport may mean that there are fewer meetings and that more work is done over the phone and through the exchange of letters or tapes. Teleconferencing and smaller scale link ups offer scope for efficient consultation and decision making. 'I find it concentrates the mind wonderfully and increases the amount of ground that can be covered in a short time', said a disabled woman who regularly chairs tele-conferences.

There is no substitute for meeting on occasion; all the more so for volunteers who may have worked together for years at a distance without having the opportunity to meet in person. Travel, when it does occur, tends to involve greater costs; the inaccessibility of buses, coaches and most underground train routes increasing the need to use taxis or private transport, using a paid driver.

Some, though by no means all, disabled volunteers carry out their commitments within the context of ill health. Energy levels can be low or unpredictable, or the need may arise for unforeseen hospital trips, treatment or simply for rest. The fact that volunteers may need to withdraw, whether temporarily or permanently, at short notice, underlines what is actually true of any voluntary organisation; that it is not good practice to depend too much upon the contribution of any one individual. A 'buddy' system, in which individual volunteers maintain supportive contact with each other, and the development of 'shadow' roles, so that volunteers in key roles have back up if they need to ease-up on their involvement for any reason, have both been found to be effective strategies.

In order to do their work disabled volunteers may need to pay someone; a personal assistant, driver, reader, runner, interpreter or, in the case of a parent with learning difficulties, supporter. There are cost implications to be faced, though funders are increasingly demonstrating that they understand the importance of this.

Matching the needs of individual volunteers and groups to appropriate technological resources is a key area of potential. Many of the latest developments in information technology have scope for facilitating both the work of disabled volunteers and the contact between them – the use of voice-activated word processors, speech software, E-mail, fax machines and teleconferencing facilities, for example. However, because disabled volunteers do not represent a lucrative commercial market it can be difficult to track down information about what is available and to finance the choices once they have been made.

Organisations of disabled people are not necessarily better at inclusive practice than others. Sending out information in formats suited to all who receive it and holding meetings in venues and along lines which enable all to participate, can pull on resources which are already stretched. In practice, access does not always remain a priority. But disabled people, and increasingly those who fund them, recognise the importance of such actions, both in terms of the solidarity between people whose impairments may be different but who share a common lack of opportunity and in terms of providing a model for others to learn from.

Organisations that have enlisted the expertise of disabled parent volunteers in working groups (for example the National Childbirth Trust and Maternity Alliance) report that they have benefited from the way it has brought the issue of accessibility to the fore and made the whole of the organisation more inclusive in its practice.

PARENTS AS VOLUNTEERS

Parents with commitments to groups or organisations have to juggle these with other demands on their time; the regular household tasks such as shopping, housework, cooking, pick-ups from school, etc and also the unforeseen demands – a child who comes home from school in need of attention, a partner struggling to meet a deadline at work, the broken washing machine and so on.

Being practised in the skill of juggling can be a great asset in a volunteer and should not necessarily be perceived as a problem at all. It does however call for flexibility and responsiveness on the part of the group or organisation, as well as the volunteer. For example, in the National Childbirth Trust, an organisation in which every volunteer is also a parent, contact lists include details of the times when each person on the list prefers to be contacted and the times that they should not be contacted.

The arrival of a new baby inevitably calls for major and continuing readjustments in the lives of volunteers. Around the birth and in the first few months it is obvious to everyone that a new mother will need to remove herself altogether from the action for a period of time. It is never possible to predict in advance how long the period of withdrawal will be, as there are so many variables to be taken into account. The difficulty for volunteers is that whereas arrangements for maternity leave are explicitly agreed and formalised in the context of paid employment, volunteers can feel under pressure to resume a job that otherwise would not get done, even where this conflicts with family interests.

The scope for flexibility in voluntary work is both part of its attraction to parents and part of its difficulty. Work can be arranged to fit in with family schedules and unforeseen circumstances, yet at the same time there may be no-one to notice when the pressures are mounting up. 'Mentor' or 'buddy' systems in which volunteers regularly check out with each other how things are going can help in balancing the demands of family life and external commitments.

Paid or unpaid?

Much of the work that disabled people do is unpaid. The rigidities of the benefit system prohibit people who receive benefits from making a voluntary contribution unless it can be shown that it is 'therapeutic' in its effect on them. This seems ironic when what the disabled person is actually doing is putting in a lot of effort to benefit others. Even so, if they work more than 16 hours they are threatened with having benefits taken away.

My interviews with disabled parents suggested that many of them wanted to have work to do but were excluded from the job market by its lack of flexibility and accessibility to parents and disabled people. Some are happy to make their contribution on a voluntary basis since the work is important to them and satisfying, but many are simply not in a position to do that, if it leaves them short of money. It is essential to the involvement of many volunteers that their expenses are fully met. This includes administration, travel and childcare but it may include less obvious costs too. A disabled parent may need to employ childcare not only whilst they attend a day-long meeting but also while they rest and recover the next day.

It is important for disabled women to have the same access to opportunities for self-development as others. A voluntary organisation like the National Childbirth Trust can offer a career (albeit unpaid) to women who are precluded from the world of paid work by the inflexibility of work schedules and the distrust still shown by some employers towards women who choose to combine childcare and a career. Recognition of this does not preclude them, as disabled people and as women, from asking themselves what they are prepared to do as volunteers and what work they consider they should be paid for.

Much of the work done in support of professionals working with disabled parents has been done by parents themselves, often on a voluntary basis. This has been undertaken willingly and generally speaking has been seen as a good opportunity to influence professional practice. It is important that contributions to the training, advising and informing of professionals should be acknowledged – paying disabled parents for their contribution is one way of demonstrating that their expertise is valued. It also helps to ensure that whilst professionals are able to draw on the expertise and resources offered by disabled parents, this is not done at the personal expense of volunteers and does not compromise the priority that the network of disabled parents has, to give support to its own members.

Some of the most relevant, up-to-date and practical information available to disabled parents is that which comes from other disabled parents. Local self-help groups and a national network play a vital role in information dissemination and providing moral support. Peer support offered by someone in a similar situation is often highly valued. It is at the same time essential to recognise the demands that peer support can make on volunteers and the need for appropriate training.

WORKING FROM HOME

Disabled parents or social and medical professionals who phone a helpline are not necessarily aware of whether the person answering is a paid employee with an office and back-up staff or a parent with flagging energies, answering from their kitchen phone whilst preparing a meal, comforting a fallen

'Put you through to my secretary? I should be so lucky!'

child and trying to answer a knock at the door. The caller may therefore have unrealistic expectations of what that person is in a position to do for them. In its most recent information leaflet, ParentAbility took care to point out that all its work is undertaken by parent volunteers working from home.

As well as trying to give an accurate picture of what is on offer there is a need for a flexible back-up system for volunteers so that someone who is having a difficult day can leave another contact number on their answer-phone and take a break. People involved in telephone response may require training both in listening and counselling skills and also in being clear about their own limitations. Sometimes the counsellor will need someone to talk to after an emotionally-demanding encounter.

At an evaluation and planning meeting for ParentAbility's core volunteers, isolation was identified as an issue that needed tackling. Everyone was given the option of choosing for themselves another member of the core team to keep in touch with on a regular basis and who could be contacted when a listening ear was needed. Some individuals with key and demanding roles were encouraged to appoint deputies who could take over from them as and when the need arose.

Enabling strategies such as those described in this section of the book are essential. Without them no attempt to set up self-help networks can succeed, for only those who are economically well-off and socially privileged would be able to contribute and so the strengths inherent in genuine peer support would be lost.

POWER THROUGH PARTICIPATION

The coming together of disabled parents is one strand in what Michael Oliver has identified as a national and international movement of self-actualization and empowerment amongst disabled people.[1] The movement from passively experiencing disadvantage through to actively contributing to its elimination is a powerful transformation in the lives of individuals and in society as a whole.

At the heart of this movement lies an insight which is also at the heart of this book; beyond the desire to be seen as normal and beyond the desire to join in at any cost lies the recognition of our value as the people we are and our collective power to bring about change.

What happens to the desire 'to live as normal a life as possible' once disabled parents have come together, countered the sense of isolation and exposure which made it seem unsafe to be different and take on the task of self representation? Does it fall away? Well yes and no. Yes, in the sense that it leaves them free, as they wished, to get on with the pains and the pleasures of day-to-day living with their children. Yes, in the sense that they are relieved of the effort of seeking to justify themselves in 'able-bodied' terms and yes, in the sense that they can take full pride in living life the way they do. No, in the sense that so long as disabled people remain amongst the poorest and have little or no redress in law against unfair discrimination, they will not be able to participate as fully as they would choose in the range of activities and options open to other, non-disabled, parents.

We no longer accept to see ourselves as a sub-group of parents at risk who somehow got through the net and had better watch our step. We had a right to become parents in the first place and we have the right to be adequately and appropriately resourced in the task. We are ordinary parents and at the same time we have particular insights and qualities which we have developed in our parenting. We are on our way. Are you sure *you* can cope?

Notes

INTRODUCTION

1. Goodman, M 1994: see Maternity Alliance Disability Working Group 1994: 1.
2. French, A 1989: *I, Alison.* p.35.
3. French, S 1993: 'Redefining disability: a challenge to research'. In Swain, J, Finkelstein, V, French, S and Oliver, M (eds) *Disabling barriers – enabling environments.* p.63.
4. Booth, T and Booth, W 1994: *Parenting under pressure: Mothers and fathers with learning difficulties.* p.13.
5. Morris, J (ed) 1993: *Independent lives?: community care and disabled people.* p.63.
6. IBID, 1993, p.75.
7. Maternity Alliance 1994: 'Love over muscle'. *Maternity Action* 64, April/May/June.
8. Goodman, M 1994: see Maternity Alliance Disability Working Group 1994: 1.
9. Campion, M J 1995: *Who's fit to be a parent?*
10. Goodman, M 1994: see Maternity Alliance Disability Working Group 1994: 1.
11. Wates, M 1993: 'Righting the picture: images of disabled parents', *Disability, Pregnancy & Parenthood International* 2, April: 2–3.
12. See Dyer, C 1991: 'Consent for operations on the mentally handicapped', *British Medical Journal*, 302, 16 February: 373; also a recent newspaper report in *The Times* 5 October 1995: 'Abortion order on handicap girl, 17'. (National Childbirth Trust 1990 (1984): *The emotions and*

experiences of some mothers with disabilities. Updated from 1984; Shackle, M 1994: see Maternity Alliance Disability Working Group 1994: 2.

13. Carers National Association 1993: *Young Carer,* November.

14. ParentAbility 1991: *Accessible birth: a ParentAbility report on physical access to maternity units by parents with disabilities.*

15. National Childbirth Trust 1990 (1984): *The emotions and experiences of some mothers with disabilities.* Updated from 1984.

16. Finger, A 1988: *Past due.*

17. Campion, M J 1990: *The baby challenge: a handbook on pregnancy for women with a physical disability.*

18. Maternity Alliance Disability Working Group 1994.

19. Rieser, R and Mason, M 1992: *Disability equality in the classroom: a human rights issue* (revised edition).

20. Morris, J (ed) 1989: *Able lives: women's experience of paralysis.*

21. Keith, L 1994: *Mustn't grumble . . .: writing by disabled women.*

22. Morris, J (ed) 1992: *Alone together: voices of single mothers.*

23. Campion, M J 1995: *Who's fit to be a parent?*

24. Wilkins, V 1995: *Are we there yet?* and *Boots for a bridesmaid.*

25. Zarb, G (ed) 1995: *Removing disabling barriers.* p.97.

CHAPTER ONE: NOT ANOTHER BOOK ABOUT HEROINES

1. National Childbirth Trust 1990 (1984): *The emotions and experiences of some mothers with disabilities.* Updated from 1984.

2. Strauss, A L *et al.*: *Chronic illness and the quality of life* (second edition). 1984

3. Voysey, M 1975: *A constant burden: the reconstitution of family life.*

4. Sutherland, A 1981: *Disabled we stand.*

5. Morris, J (ed) 1991: *Pride against prejudice: transforming attitudes to disability.*

6. Abberley, P 1993: 'Disabled people and normality'. In Swain, J, Finkelstein, V, French, S and Oliver, M (eds) *Disabling barriers – enabling environments.*

7. Campbell, J and Oliver, M 1996: *Disability politics: understanding our past, changing our future.*

8. IMPAIRMENT lacking part or all of a limb, or having a defective limb, organism or mechanism of the body; DISABILITY the disadvantage or restriction of activity caused by a contemporary social organisation which takes little or no account of people who have physical impairments and thus excludes them from the mainstream of social activities. (The Union of the Physically Impaired Against Segregation, 76: 3–4) Quoted in Oliver, M 1990: *The politics of disablement.*

9. Swain, J, Finkelstein, V, French, S and Oliver, M (eds) *Disabling barriers – enabling environments.*

CHAPTER FOUR: THE CHILDREN

1. Three publications which focus on the experience of the *children* of disabled parents are Grimshaw, R 1992: *Children of parents with Parkinson's disease;* Bilsborrow, S 1992: 'You grow up fast as well': *Young carers in Merseyside;* and Segal, J and Simkins, J 1993: *My mum needs me: helping children with ill or disabled parents.*

2. MS Society 1989: *Has your mum or dad got ms?*

3. Meredith, H 1992: 'Supporting the young carer', *Community Outlook,* May, 16.

CHAPTER FIVE: SELF-IMAGE

1. Finkelstein, V 1993. In Swain, J, Finkelstein, V, French, S and Oliver, M (eds) Disabling barriers – enabling environments. p14.

2. ParentAbility 1993: *What parents find helpful and*

unhelpful: pregnancy and parenthood for people with learning difficulties.

CHAPTER SIX: BEING ON THE EDGE AND BEING INVOLVED

1. Titmuss, R M 1970: *The gift relationship: from human blood to social policy.*

CHAPTER SEVEN: 'YOU SHOULDN'T HAVE TO FIGHT'

1. Craske, A and Wodynska, R 1994: 'Backing the expert: enabling parents to meet their personal assistance needs', *Disability, Pregnancy & Parenthood International*, 6, April 2 – 4.
2. Morris, J (ed) 1993: *Independent lives?: community care and disabled people.* pp168 – 9.

CHAPTER EIGHT: ALLIES

1. Morris, J (ed) 1993: Independent Lives?: community care and disabled people.
2. Parents Too! Project proposal, August 1996.
3. Department of Health 1993: *Changing childbirth.*
4. Morris, J (ed) 1992: *Alone together: voices of single mothers.*

CHAPTER NINE: MEETING

1. PANDA 1995: *Families first: a study of disabled parents of school-aged children and their families.*
2. Wates, M and Saunders, K 1993: *Disabled mothers: supporting each other.*
3. Crewe, N and and Zola, I 1983: *Independent living for physically disabled people.*pp xii–xiv, quoted in Oliver, M 1990: *The politics of disablement.*
4. MADWG, 1994: See Maternity Alliance Disability Working Group 1994: 3.

Chapter Ten: Developing a self-help network

1. National Childbirth Trust 1990 (1984): *The emotions and experiences of some mothers with disabilities.* Updated from 1984.

2. IBID, 1990 (1984).

3. Society of Community Medicine.

4. Disabled Living Foundation.

5. Multiple Sclerosis Society.

6. National Childbirth Trust 1990 (1984): *The emotions and experiences of some mothers with disabilities.* Updated from 1984, p.36.

7. ParentAbility 1991: Accessible birth: a ParentAbility report on physical access to maternity units by parents with disabilities.

8. ParentAbility 1994: *Accessible health: a ParentAbility survey of access to primary health services in the UK.*

9. ParentAbility 1996: New Generation and Digest 15 (2): *Results of a survey on access to peer group activities.*

10. ParentAbility 1994: *Resource list: a ParentAbility guide to pregnancy, birth and parenthood for people with disabilities.*

11. Shackle, M 1994: see Maternity Alliance Disability Working Group 1994: 2, p.13.

12. MADWG 1994: see Maternity Alliance Disability Working Group 1994: 3.

13. Department of Health 1993: *Changing childbirth.*

14. Goodman, M 1994: see Maternity Alliance Disability Working Group 1994: 1.

15. Shackle, M 1994: see Maternity Alliance Disability Working Group 1994: 2.

16. MADWG 1994: see Maternity Alliance Disability Working Group 1994: 3.

17. Campion, M J 1990: *The baby challenge: a handbook on pregnancy for women with physical disabilities.*

18. Campion, M J 1995: *Who's fit to be a parent?*

19. ParentAbility 1993: *What parents find helpful and unhelpful and parenthood for people with learning difficulties.*

20. National Childbirth Trust 1990 (1984): *The emotions and experiences of some mothers with disabilities*. Updated from 1984.

CHAPTER ELEVEN: POWER THROUGH PARTICIPATION

1. Oliver, M 1990: *The politics of disablement* p119.

Bibliography

Abberley, P 1993: 'Disabled people and normality'. In Swain, J, Finkelstein, V, French, S and Oliver, M (eds) *Disabling barriers – enabling environments*. [Full ref. see separate entry]

Barnes, C 1991: *Disabled people in Britain and discrimination: a case for anti-discrimination legislation*. Hurst, London.

Bilsborrow, S 1992: *'You grow up fast as well': Young carers in Merseyside*. Barnardos, Ilford.

Booth, T and Booth, W 1994: *Parenting under pressure: mothers and fathers with learning difficulties*. Open University Press, Buckingham and Philadelphia.

Campbell, J and Oliver, M 1996: *Disability politics: understanding our past, changing our future*. Routledge, London and New York.

Campion, M J 1990: *The baby challenge: a handbook on pregnancy for women with a physical disability*. Tavistock/Routledge, London and New York.

–1995: *Who's fit to be a parent?* Routledge, London and New York.

Carers National Association 1993: *Young Carer*, November, Carers National Association, London.

Counsell, A 1982: *So clear in my mind*. Hutchinson.

Craske, A & Wodynska, R 1994: 'Backing the expert: enabling parents to meet their personal assistance needs', *Disability, Pregnancy & Parenthood International*, 6, April: 2–4.

Crewe, N and Zola, I 1983: *Independent living for physically disabled people*. Jossey-Bass, London.

Department of Health 1993: *Changing childbirth*. HMSO, London.

Dyer, C 1991: 'Consent for operations on the mentally handicapped', *British Medical Journal*, 302, 16 February: 373.

Finger, A 1988: *Past due*. The Women's Press, London.

French, A 1989: *I, Alison*. Victor Gollancz, London.

French, S 1993: 'Redefining disability: a challenge to research'. In Swain, J, Finkelstein, V, French S and Oliver, M (eds) *Disabling barriers – enabling environments*.

Goodman, M 1994: See Maternity Alliance Disability Working Group 1994: 1.

Graham, J 1996: *Multiple sclerosis: pregnancy and parenthood*. MS Resource Centre, Stansted.

Grimshaw, R 1992: *Children of parents with Parkinson's disease*. National Children's Bureau, London.

Keith, L 1994: *Mustn't grumble . . . : writing by disabled women*. The Women's Press, London.

MADWG 1994: See Maternity Alliance Disability Working Group 1994: 3

Maternity Alliance 1994: 'Love over muscle'. *Maternity Action* 64, April/May/June.

Maternity Alliance Disability Working Group 1994. A pack consisting of:

1. Goodman, M: *Mothers' pride and others' prejudice*. Results of a national survey of disabled mothers' experiences of maternity.

2. Shackle, M: *I thought I was the only one*. Report of a 1992 conference, 'Disabled People, Pregnancy and Early Parenthood'.

3. MADWG: *Listen to us for a change. A charter for disabled parents and parents-to-be*.

All published by the Maternity Alliance, London.

Meredith, H 1992: 'Supporting the young carer', *Community Outlook*, May, 15–18.

Morris, J (ed.) 1989: *Able lives: women's experience of paralysis*. The Women's Press, London.

–1991: *Pride against prejudice: transforming attitudes to disability*. The Women's Press, London.

–1992: *Alone together: voices of single mothers.* The Women's Press, London.

–1993: *Independent lives?: community care and disabled people.* Macmillan, Basingstoke and London.

MS Society 1989: *Has your mum or dad got MS?* London.

National Childbirth Trust 1990 (1984): *The emotions and experiences of some mothers with disabilities.* Updated from 1984, National Childbirth Trust, London.

Oliver, M 1990: *The politics of disablement.* Macmillan, Basingstoke and London.

–1993: 'Redefining disability: a challenge to research'. In Swain, J, Finkelstein, V, French S and Oliver, M (eds) *Disabling barriers – enabling environments.*

PANDA 1995: *Families first: a study of disabled parents of school-aged children and their families.* PANDA (Association of Disabled Parents in the Norfolk Area).

ParentAbility 1991: *Accessible birth: a ParentAbility report on physical access to maternity units by parents with disabilities.* National Childbirth Trust, London.

–1993: *What parents find helpful and unhelpful: pregnancy and parenthood for people with learning difficulties.* National Childbirth Trust, London.

–1994: *Accessible health: a ParentAbility survey of access to primary health services in the UK.* National Childbirth Trust, London.

–1994: *Resource list: a ParentAbility guide to pregnancy, birth and parenthood for people with disabilities.* National Childbirth Trust, London.

–1996: New Generation and Digest 15 (2): *Results of a survey on access to peer group activities.*

Parents Too! 1995: 16 June press release. RADAR, London.

Rieser, R and Mason, M 1992: *Disability equality in the classroom: a human rights issue.* Disability Equality in Education, London. First published by the Inner London Education Authority.

Saxton, M and Howe, F 1988: *With wings: an anthology of literature by women with disabilities.* Virago Press, London.

155

Segal, J and Simkins, J 1993: *My mum needs me: helping children with ill or disabled parents*. Penguin, Harmondsworth.

Shackle, M 1994: See Maternity Alliance Disability Working Group 1994: 2.

Small, E 1992: 'Growing up fast', *Social Work Today*, Birmingham, 7 May.

Strauss A L *et al.* 1984: *Chronic illness and the quality of life* (second edition). C V Mosby, St. Louis.

Sutherland A 1981: *Disabled we stand*. Souvenir, London.

Swain, J, Finkelstein, V, French S and Oliver, M (eds) 1993: *Disabling barriers – enabling environments*. Sage, London, Thousand Oaks and New Delhi, in association with The Open University.

Titmuss, R M 1970: *The gift relationship: from human blood to social policy*. Allen & Unwin, London.

Voysey, M 1975: *A constant burden: the reconstitution of family life*. Routledge and Kegan Paul, London and Boston.

Wates, M 1991: 'Able parents – disability, pregnancy and motherhood', *Maternity Action* 52 (9).

–1993: 'Righting the picture: images of disabled parents', *Disability, Pregnancy & Parenthood International* 2, April: 2–3.

–1994: 'However will you cope?', *New Generation* 13, December: 12–13.

Wates, M and Saunders, K 1993: *Disabled mothers: supporting each other*. Women's Health, London.

Wilkins, V 1995: *Are we there yet?* and *Boots for a bridesmaid*. UK Spinal Injuries Association in collaboration with Tamarind Books.

Zarb, G (ed.) 1995: *Removing disabling barriers*. Policy Studies Institute.

Useful Organisations

Disabled Parent Support Groups There are a number of local support groups around the country. ParentAbility seeks to maintain an up-to-date list.

PANDA Association of Disabled Parents in the Norfolk Area, and publishers of *Families First* (see Bibliography). Contact Kathy Saunders, 145 Main Road, Clenchwarton, Kings Lynn, Norfolk PE34 4DT.

ParentAbility is a peer network supporting disabled people in pregnancy, childbirth and parenthood. Contact via the National Childbirth Trust, Alexandra House, Oldham Terrace, Acton, London W3 6NH. Tel: 0181 992 8637.

Parents Too! is a coalition of disabled parents, organisations and individuals working to promote recognition of the rights of disabled parents and empower disabled parents in getting the services, support and resources they want and need. Contact via RADAR, 12 City Forum, 250 City Road, London EC1V 8AF. Tel: 0171 250 3222.

Right From The Start A project to promote effective support for parents and prospective parents who have learning difficulties. Contact via the Maternity Alliance at the address below.

The Maternity Alliance works for improvements in rights and services for parents and babies and has a Disability Working Group with representation from a number of disabled parents and interested organisations. 5th Floor, 54 Beech Street, London EC2P 2LX. Telephone and minicom: 0171 588 8583, Information line: 0171 588 8582.

PUBLICATIONS

DPPI (Disability, Pregnancy and Parenthood International) A quarterly journal which aims to bring together expertise from both disabled parents and professionals in different parts of the world. Back copies and subscriptions (£20 per annum) from Arrowhead Productions, 1 Chiswick Staithe, Hartington Road, London W4 3TP.

ParentAbility's Resource List, a comprehensive and detailed list of information and resources, is regularly updated. Available from NCT Maternity Sales Ltd, 239 Shawbridge Street, Glasgow 43 1QN. Disability Network (01744 451215) will put the list onto tape on request.

Parents Too! is, at the time of writing, seeking funding to produce a comprehensive resource guide and rights handbook by and for disabled parents.

The Maternity Alliance Disability Working Group (MADWG) in 1994 produced a set of three linked publications concerned with disabled parents – a conference report, results of a postal survey and a charter for good practice (see Bibliography). These are available from the Maternity Alliance at the address given above.

Index